BROKEN

TIMELINES

BOOK 1: EGYPT

JACK STORNOWAY

Copyright

While every precaution has been taken in the preparation of this book, the publisher assumes no responsibility for errors or omissions, or for damages resulting from the use of the information contained herein.

BROKEN TIMELINES - BOOK 1: EGYPT

First edition. December 27, 2019

Copyright © 2019 Jack Stornoway

ISBN: 978-1990289910

Table of Contents

TABLE OF CONTENTS

Introduction

Egypt is unique among Earth's ancient cultures, as the Egyptians kept records longer than most cultures existed. Around 300 BC the Egyptian historian Manetho compiled a record of Egyptian History for the Greeks. It was the height of Greek cultural influence. The Greeks were ruling everything from southern Italy to northwest India, and had established colonies as far west as France, and as far north as Crimea. Manetho's book Aegyptiaca, circulated far and wide within the Greek world, and then the Roman and Sassanian Empires that rose up to consume the Greek world. Within Aegyptiaca, the dynastic history of Egypt was divided into 30 dynasties, the same dynasties Egyptologists use today. Manetho was the first to refer to the ancient Egyptian royal families as dynasties, however, his account matches the Turin King List dating to the New Kingdom era a thousand years earlier and is believed to be an accurate account of what the Egyptians of his period believed. The Turin King List only listed the kings and queens up until the time of the New Kingdom, and Manetho only listed the kings and queens up until the last independent Egyptian royal family. Subsequently, the 31st Dynasty was added, which was the last Persian period of rule, which was followed by the Greek and Roman eras.

While Manetho and modern Egyptologists do agree on the general outline of Egyptian history, there are some striking differences, modern Egyptologists have removed over a hundred kings from Manetho's timeline, compressing Egyptian history from a dynastic period that should have started in

5510 BC, to a dynastic period that starts in 3100 BC. There are also ongoing efforts to change the foundation date of the 1st Dynasty of Egypt to 3000 BC (Ian Shaw) or 2770 BC (David Rohl). These ongoing attempts to revise Egyptian 'history' create more and more fictional history, as dynasties are either forced to coexist or erases them entirely from the timeline. Manetho's 7th Dynasty is now considered fictitious by Egyptologists,[1] even though it was mentioned in the Turin King List, and the names of the kings were recorded in the Abydos King Lists, both lists dating from the New Kingdom era.

The problem with constantly compressing Egyptian history is that it forces all neighboring civilizations' history to also become compressed or else leaves massive anachronisms, such as the currently accepted, yet absolutely impossible fact that ancient Sumerians were using horses and war-chariots 1000 years before the Egyptians. This would be like the French inventing biplanes in the Middle Ages and everyone else figuring it out in the 1900s. France would have conquered the world if they have biplanes in the Middle Ages, and Sumer would have conquered Egypt during the First Egyptian Dark Age (First Intermediate Period), if the Sumerians had war-chariots while the Egyptians were running around on foot. This anachronism is epitomized in the Middle Kingdom expeditions into Canaan circa 1870 BC, which would have encountered horses as they had been in use in the Middle East since at least 2550 BC, yet none of the Egyptians bothered noting

---

[1] Toby Wilkinson (2010) "Timeline," *The Rise and Fall of Ancient Egypt*

it, or commenting on how they conquered the locals, who would have in fact defeated the Egyptians if the Canaanites actually had horses during Senusret III's invasion.

The anachronisms become even worse when the Hyksos appear on the border of Egypt around 1674 BC, invading with horses, war-chariots, and composite bows. The Hyksos introduce these technologies to Egypt, but where did they come from? The Egyptians recorded that the Hyksos occupied Byblos in Canaan before marching south into Egypt, yet none of the Middle Eastern nations noticed. Not Byblos trading partners of Qatna (Southern Syria), Yamhad (Northern Syria), not the Hittite Empire (Central Turkey), not the Assyrian Empire (Northern Iraq), and not the Babylonian Empire (Southern Iraq). To complicate the situation the Hyksos were a largely Semitic people, with a Hurrian nobility who for some reason occasionally had Indo-Aryan names. There simply were no such people in the Middle East when the Hyksos invaded Egypt, but there would be a century later, after Babylonia fell, and the Mitanni Empire emerged. To make things worse when the Egyptians drove them out circa 1535 BC, they simply vanished at the Egyptian border. Manetho recorded that 480,000 Hyksos were driven from Egypt, yet no one in the Middle East noticed.

The only way to believe the Conventional Egyptian Timeline (CET) is to accept that the Hyksos were time-travelers. And now, we're on the verge of cutting another century or more out of the CET, meaning even more anachronisms will appear. How has this been allowed to happen?

Part 1 - Dynastic Egypt

The purpose of this work is to demonstrate that the original Egyptian timeline, as recorded by Manetho and the ancient Egyptian King Lists, and as documented by the foremost Egyptologist of the British Empire, Sir W. M. Flinders Petrie, actually make far more sense than the CET. The original timeline is herein called the Unified Long Timeline (ULT) as it also takes into account the dynastic records of Mesopotamia, and the various lines of scientific evidence amassed in the past century such as dendrochronology, paleoclimatology, and carbondating.

The dates used in the ULT are taken from Petrie's *Researches In Sinai* from 1906, and should not be misconstrued as exact dates. Petrie himself states that the earlier dates could be up to a century off, due to the limited amounts of records and artifacts dating to the Old and Middle Kingdoms. Likewise, the CET used herein is the 'Middle Chronology' of Egyptology. Egyptologists have worked out several variations of the short timeline, with each generation seeming to want to distinguish itself by erasing more of Egypt's ancient history. And it is history, it was written down. There were Kings and Queens recorded, yet the way Egyptologists are going, by the year 3000, the Great Pyramids of Giza will probably have been designed by Archimedes and built by Cleopatra. The various versions of the CET proposed the past century can deviate by up to 630 years for the foundation of the 1st Dynasty, therefore the CET dates given should also be considered relative.

PART 1 - DYNASTIC EGYPT

The following is a comparison between the two timelines:

DYNASTIC EGYPTIAN TIMELINES			
Period	**Dynasty**	**CET**	**ULT**
Early Dynastic Era	1st	3100 to 2890 BC	5510 to 5247 BC
	2nd	2890 to 2686 BC	5247 to 4945 BC
Old Kingdom	3rd	2686 to 2613 BC	4945 to 4731 BC
	4th	2613 to 2498 BC	4731 to 4454 BC
	5th	2498 to 2384 BC	4454 to 4206 BC
	6th	2384 to 2181 BC	4206 to 4003 BC
First Egyptian Dark Age (First Intermediate Period)	7th		4003 to 3933 BC
	8th	2181 to 2160 BC	3922 to 3787 BC
	9th	2160 to 2130 BC	3787 to 3687 BC
	10th	2130 to 2040 BC	3687 to 3502 BC

PART 1 - DYNASTIC EGYPT

DYNASTIC EGYPTIAN TIMELINES			
Period	**Dynasty**	**CET**	**ULT**
Middle Kingdom	11th	2061 to 1991 BC	3502 to 3459 BC
	12th	1991 to 1803 BC	3459 to 3246 BC
Second Egyptian Dark Age (Second Intermediate Period)	13th	1803 to 1649 BC	3246 to 2793 BC
	14th	1704 to 1690 BC	2793 to 2533 BC
	15th	1674 to 1535 BC	2533 to 2249 BC
	16th	1660 to 1600 BC	2249 to 1731 BC
	Abydos	1650 to 1600 BC	
	17th	1580 to 1549 BC	1731 to 1580 BC
New Kingdom	18th	1549 to 1292 BC	1580 to 1322 BC
	19th	1292 to 1189 BC	1322 to 1202 BC
	20th	1189 to 1077 BC	1202 to 1102 BC

PART 1 - DYNASTIC EGYPT

Dynastic Egyptian Timelines			
Period	**Dynasty**	**CET**	**ULT**
Third Egyptian Dark Age (Third Intermediate Period)	21st	1069 to 945 BC	1102 to 952 BC
	22nd	943 to 716 BC	952 to 755 BC
	23rd	837 to 728 BC	755 to 721 BC
	24th	732 to 720 BC	721 to 715 BC
	25th	744 to 656 BC	715 to 644 BC
Late Period	26th	672 to 525 BC	664 to 525 BC
	27th	525 to 404 BC	
	28th	404 to 398 BC	
	29th	398 to 380 BC	
	30th	380 to 343 BC	
	31st	343 to 332 BC	
Greek Period	Argead	332 to 310 BC	
	Ptolemaic	310 to 30 BC	

Conventional View of Ancient Egypt

Open any history book today and turn to the Egyptian civilization and you'll see pretty much the same thing: the Kingdom of Egypt was founded around 3100 BC. If you go one step further and open a book on Egyptology you'll see scholarly debates about when it was exactly, with some radical Egyptologists claiming it was as early as 3400 BC, or as recent as 2770 BC. The way Egyptian history is presented it would seem that around 5000 years ago the Egyptian civilization was founded by nomadic tribes that suddenly decided to settle down somewhere.

These settlers built pens for their livestock and started farming the local grains. They then built some mud huts, and eventually through some inspired genius, invented writing, first as simple pictures, and then as more and more highly complex hieroglyphs. This no doubt led to discovering mathematics, geometry, and as their mud huts got bigger, architecture and engineering. Finally, some egotistical king decided he needed a private mountain to be buried in and worked thousands of slaves to death building the first pyramid.

Other kings decided they needed bigger and bigger pyramids, working more and more slaves to death until some slaves rebelled. Jews, Christians, and Muslims have holy books that describe a rebel from the house of Pharaoh named Moses, who unleashed ten plagues upon Egypt, causing widespread death and destruction to the point that the king let the slaves go. Then the Egyptians stopped building pyramids, probably because they didn't have enough slaves, and their civilization slowly withered until Alexander the Great invaded. After that, the Egyptian civilization ceased to exist, as the country was ruled by a series of foreign cultures starting with the Greeks, and then the Romans, Arabs, Turks, and British, before emerging as the country it is today.

While the history from the conquest of Alexander onward is essentially correct, almost everything described in the two paragraphs above prior to Alexander is fundamentally wrong. Egyptologists reading the above paragraphs might be surprised that anyone could believe such nonsense, yet many intelligent and educated people believe what is stated above. The above description of Egyptian history is so widespread, that when paleo-climatologists discovered proof of the 5.9 Kiloyear Event, it was suggested that this was what caused the nomadic tribes to settle in the Nile region. The 5.9 Kiloyear Event was an intense period of atmospheric drying and the expansion of deserts across North Africa. Before this event, much of what is today the Sahara Desert was grasslands and forests. The event happened around 5900 years ago and is linked to many human migrations that happened at the time. Naturally one of these migrations would have been out of the Sahara into the Nile River valley.

As Egyptologists all seem to agree that Egyptian civilization was founded sometime after 5900 years ago the concept has begun to gain acceptance within the Egyptology community. The idea that the 5.9 Kiloyear Event is what forced the nomadic tribes to settle in the Nile and become farmers certainly seems valid unless one asks why the virtually identical 8.2 Kiloyear Event didn't do the same thing 2300 years earlier? The answer, of course, is the circular logic that Egyptian civilization developed after the 5.9 Kiloyear Event because Egypt appears in the archaeological record starting sometime between 5400 and 4770 years ago. But did it?

Early Egyptology

This idea that Egypt was founded around 3100 BC is a fairly new idea, it has only been around for about a century. The founders of Egyptology generally claimed that Egypt was thousands of years older. Modern Egyptology began in the early 1800s when Jean-François Champollion first deciphered Egyptian hieroglyphs and set off a period of Egyptomania in Post-Napoleonic Europe. Champollion and another linguist and founder of Egyptology, Ippolito Rosellini, organized the Franco-Tuscan Expedition to Egypt of 1828-29, which greatly expanded the number of ancient Egyptian records Europeans had to study. Champollion was convinced from his translations of the ancient dynastic records, that Egypt was founded in 5867 BC.

Many early Egyptologists studying the ancient Egyptian dynastic records came to similar dates, such as Georg Friedrich Unger who in 1867 published the date of 5613 BC for the foundation of Egypt.[2] In 1904 Eduard Meyer discovered the Sothic Cycle of Heliacal Risings of Sirius, which forms the bases for the traditional timeline of Egypt, and placed the foundation date for Egypt at no later than 3315 BC. Meyer revolutionized the way Egyptologists were dating ancient Egyptian events by introducing so-called 'approximate dates,' which dealt with the gaps in Egyptian history by grouping together events that were known to have happened in relation to each other, and then dating them to the latest possible point they could have taken place according to the ancient Egyptian use of the Sothic cal-

---

[2] Georg Friedrich Unger (1867) *Chronologie des Manetho*

endar. This meant that events could have happened earlier than Meyer's dates, but not later.

Sir Flinders Petrie, who was the first chair of Egyptology in the United Kingdom, placed the foundation of Egypt at 5510 BC in his 1906 book *Researches In Sinai*. Petrie was a pioneer of systematic methodology in archaeology, the preservation of artifacts, and led many excavations of the most important archaeological sites in Egypt. Until his death in 1933, Petrie continued to be an advocate for the long timeline of Egyptian history, even as the world of Egyptology slowly shifted towards the now ubiquitous short timeline. In Petrie's own words:

> *"If any one wishes to abandon these dates, they must also abandon the greater part of the information that we have, cast Manetho and the Turin papyrus aside, ignore the evidence of Cretan archaeology, and treat history as a mere matter of arbitrary will, regardless of all records. As against this general position of dates there is nothing to be set in favour of any very different schemes, nothing — except the weightiest thing of all - prepossessions."[3]*

So what happened?

---

[3] W. M. Flinders Petrie (1906) *Researches in Sinai*, Chapter 12

Ancient Egyptology

The question 'How old is Egypt?' is not a new question. The oldest known archaeological digs in Egypt actually date back to the time of ancient Egypt. King Thutmose IV, who reigned around 1400 BC was famous for the restoration of the Sphinx at Giza, and then erecting the Dream Stele, between the two paws of the Sphinx. Around 1250 BC King Ramesses II's son Khaemweset, famously excavated and restored many historic buildings, tombs, temples, and pyramids. Prince Khaemweset is often described as 'the First Egyptologist' due to his efforts in discovering and restoring historic buildings. Restoration texts from Khaemweset have been found associated with the pyramid of Unas at Saqqara, the tomb of Shepseskaf called the Mastabat al-Fir'aun, the Sun-Temple of Nyuserre Ini, the Pyramid of Sahure, the Pyramid of Djoser, and the Pyramid of Userkaf.

For someone who has never studied the history of Egypt, the idea that the ancient Egyptians were discovering and restoring the ruins of ancient Egypt might seem strange. It is important to remember that whenever Egypt was founded, it was around for a very long time. King Thutmose IV and Prince Khaemweset lived during the period of Egyptian history known as the New Kingdom, while the buildings they were discovering and restoring dated back at least a thousand years earlier to the Old Kingdom.

Both the ULT and CET agree that the New Kingdom existed between approximately 1580 to 1102 BC ULT or 1549 to 1077 BC CET. The two timelines disagree over what happened before the New Kingdom.

The generally accepted CET places the Old Kingdom between 2686 and 2181 BC, while the ULT places the Old Kingdom between 4945 and 4003 BC. Specific versions of both timelines may differ by several hundred years when discussing the Old Kingdom.

Regardless of the timeline used, King Thutmose II and Prince Khaemweset lived at least a thousand years after the buildings they were discovering and restoring were originally built, and possibly several thousand years. It seems likely that the two ancient Egyptologists would have believed it had been several thousand years, and not just one thousand years, as the Abydos King List was created during the same era, and matches closely the timeline worked out by Manetho over a thousand years later. The Abydos King List is a list of the names of seventy-six kings of ancient Egypt, found on a wall of the Temple of Seti I at Abydos, and dated to around 1270 BC.

The ancient Egyptians kept many lists of their kings, however, each list reflects the bias of whoever wrote it. For example, the Abydos King List omits kings the priests of Abydos found heretical, such as Akhenaten, and the entire Hyksos Dynasty. This abundance of lists that only partially agree with each other is what has caused the multitude of variations of both the long and short-timelines. This plethora of histories was discovered by the Greeks when they ruled Egypt and was tackled by the Egyptian historian Manetho around 300 BC when he compiled and published *Aegyptiaca*. *Aegyptiaca*, which means 'History of Egypt' in Greek was the seminal work on Egyptian history during the Greco-Roman period.

The influence of Manetho on Egyptology cannot be understated. For two thousand years, historians and Egyptologists believed that Manetho had been the first to organize the ancient kings and queens of Egypt into the dynasties we still use today. Unfortunately, the late Roman era was fraught with religious controversies, one of which was the age of the world, as the early Christians believed that humanity was only created in 5509 BC, while the Rabbinical Jews believed it was in 3750 BC, and the Samaritans believed it happened around 4400 BC. Yet the Egyptians and Babylonians both claimed their civilizations were older than any of those dates. Early Christian theologians attacked the works of ancient historians like Manetho and Berossos, claiming that both Egypt and Babylonia had to date to after the Great Flood of Noah, which happened circa 3000 BC according to the original Greek translation of the Old Testament called the Septuagint.

Eusebius, the 'Father of Church History' wrote the following first draft of the short timeline around 300 AD, quoting and then deconstructing Manetho's Aegyptiaca in order to prove the 'Hebrew timeline':

"Excerpted from the Eusebius' Chronica

BOOK I.

Reign of Spirits and Followers of Horus

Dynasties of Gods, Demigods, and Spirits of the Dead.

From the Egyptian History of Manetho, who composed his account in three books. These deal with the Gods, the Demigods, the Spirits of the Dead, and the mortal kings who ruled Egypt down to Darius, king of the Persians.

1. The first man [or god] in Egypt is Hephaestus [Ptah], who is also renowned among the Egyptians as the discoverer of fire. His son, Helios [Ra], was succeeded by Sosis [Shu]: then follow, in turn, Cronos [Geb], Osiris, Typhon [Set], brother of Osiris, and lastly Orus [Horus], son of Osiris and Isis, These were the first to hold sway in Egypt. Thereafter, the kingship passed from one to another in unbroken succession down to Bydis through 13,900 years. The year I take, however, to be a lunar one, consisting, that is, of 30 days : what we now call a month the Egyptians used formerly to style a year.

2. After the Gods, Demigods reigned for 1255 years, and again another line of kings held sway for 1817 years: then came thirty more kings of Memphis, reigning for 1790 years; and then again ten kings of This [Thinis], reigning for 350 years.

3. There followed the rule of Spirits of the Dead and Demigods, for 5813 years.

4. The total [of the last five groups] amounts to 11,000 years, these however being lunar periods, or months. But, in truth, the whole rule of which the Egyptians tell - the rule of Gods, Demigods, and Spirits of the Dead - is reckoned to have comprised in all 24,900 lunar years, which make 2206 solar years.

5. Now, if you care to compare these figures with Hebrew timeline, you will find that they are in perfect harmony. Egypt is called Mestraim by the Hebrews; and Mestraim lived not long after the Flood. For after the Flood, Cham (or Ham), son of Noah, begat Aegyptus or Mestraim, who was the first to set out to establish himself in Egypt, at the time when the

tribes began to disperse this way and that. Now the whole time from Adam to the Flood was, according to the Hebrews, 2242 years.

6. But, since the Egyptians claim by a sort of prerogative of antiquity that they have, before the Flood, a line of Gods, Demigods, and Spirits of the Dead, who reigned for more than 20,000 years, it clearly follows that these years should be reckoned as the same number of months as the years recorded by the Hebrews: that is, that all the months contained in the Hebrew record of years, should be reckoned as so many lunar years of the Egyptian calculation, in accordance with the total length of time reckoned from the creation of man in the beginning down to Mestraim. Mestraim was indeed the founder of the Egyptian race; and from him the first Egyptian dynasty must be held to spring.

7. But if the number of years is still in excess, it must be supposed that perhaps several Egyptian kings ruled at one and the same time; for they say that the rulers were kings of This, of Memphis, of Sals, of Ethiopia, and of other places at the same time. It seems, moreover, that different kings held sway in different regions, and that each dynasty was confined to its own nome : thus it was not a succession of kings occupying the throne one after the other, but several kings reigning at the same time in different regions. Hence arose the great total number of years. But let us leave this question and take up in detail the timeline of Egyptian history."

Clearly, early Christian Egyptologists learned the lesson of Eusebius and passed it on to their secular descendants: If you don't like what the Egyptians recorded, just make something up!

Modern Egyptologists entirely reject the idea that the Egyptians didn't know the difference between months and years, the idea is so preposterous it is surprising that anyone would have bothered writing it down. It supposes that most of the ancient kings of Egypt ruled for less than a year. It's as if Eusebius had no idea how babies are made.

...but if that first idea doesn't work, no worries, maybe all the kings were around at the same time. Maybe every little village had a king. Why not? It's not like the Egyptians built anything that would require a unified government drawing on resources from across the country. This multiple concurrent dynasties hypothesis would enter Egyptology in the early 1800s, be thoroughly debunked by 1900, and then return to dominate Egyptology by the 1950s.

Dark Age Egyptology

During the European dark age that followed the fall of Rome, the question became mute as few Europeans could read, and most of the books from the pre-Christian era had been burnt. The Great Pyramids of Giza were believed by Medieval Christians to be grain silos erected by the Israelite patriarch Joseph while he was enslaved in Egypt. This strange idea of a solid stone grain silo still finds believers among Christian fundamentalists today.

In Egypt and the greater Islamic world, interest in the ancient Egyptians continued unabated. Most of the ancient Greek and Latin books that survived the Christian book burnings, only survived because copies of them were preserved in Persia and Arabia. Egyptian historians wrote extensively about the ancient Egyptian civilization, including Abdul Latif al-Baghdadi, a teacher at Cairo's Al-Azhar University around 1200 AD, and Al-Maqrizi an Egyptian historian around 1400 AD. Unfortunately, after centuries of occupation by the Nubians, Assyrians, Persians, Greeks, Romans, and Arabs, the Egyptians had lost the ability to translate hieroglyphs and hieratic. Around 900 AD the alchemist Ibn Wahshiyyah managed to partially decipher the ancient Egyptian scripts, however, it wasn't until Champollion's work in the early-1800s AD that the full translation of ancient Egyptian text became possible.

As Europe passed through the Renaissance classical Greek and Roman works began to circulate again in Europe, and historians began to question the idea that the Pyramids of the Giza plateau were used to store grain. Napoleon's invasion of Egypt inspired the imagination of Europeans, and less than a decade after Napoleon's defeat, Jean-François Champollion announced he had deciphered the ancient Egyptian hieroglyphs. For the first time in over 1000 years, humanity could read what the ancient Egyptians had written down. Expeditions were mounted to Egypt to recover as many texts and artifacts as possible. Europe had entered the age of Egyptomania, and the rape of Egypt had begun.

Champollion's translation of the ancient hieroglyphs that supported Manetho's ancient timeline re-sparked the old animosity between bible literalists and the early European Egyptologists. The conflicting dates had become even more problematic because the bibles in western Europe had been changed by the 1500s, and now the world was only 5700 years old, meaning Champollion was stating that Egypt was founded over 1800 years before God made the world!

The changes in the bibles were caused by the decision to switch from the dating used in the old Greek Septuagint to the dating used in the Masoretic Text found in the Rabbinical Jewish Tanakh. The Greek Septuagint is a translation of the ancient Hebrew scriptures that became the Old Testament of the Bible, made around 200 BC when Judea was part of the Greek world. The Masoretic Texts was a version of the same Jewish scriptures that were used by a group of Rabbis between 600 and 1000 AD, that had a different dating for the lives of the ancient patriarchs than the Septuagint. The Masoretic Texts were copied from older texts by a group of Jewish scribes called the Masoretes, and date to sometime before 400 AD, as a fragment of one was found in 1970 dating to between 210 and 390 AD.

The three competing calendars and ages of the Earth were noted by the Early Christians, who adopted the Greek Septuagint over the Rabbinical Jewish texts or Samaritan texts. Starting around 800 AD some Christian leaders began to switch to the Masoretic Text, believing they were more accurate copies of the ancient Hebrew scriptures. While this had at first been heretical, by 1500 AD almost all Old Testaments in Europe were based on translations of the Masoretic Text. During the Renaissance and Reformation, and into the Age of Enlightenment the idea that the world was created around 4000 BC was accepted as fact by almost everyone in Europe. Sir Isaac Newton, Johannes Kepler, and Martin Luther each published dates for the age of the world, ranging between 4004 and 3961 BC.

The First Egyptian Short Timeline

The second school of thought quickly developed within Egyptology, based on the premise that the Egyptians couldn't have founded their civilization before God made the world, and therefore Egyptian history could not date back further than 4004 BC. The problem was that the ancient Egyptians had records of their kings. The king lists might have been incomplete, but the combined length of the reigns the Egyptologists knew about added up to over 5000 years, ending when Alexander conquered Egypt in 332 BC. The early advocates of the short timeline decided to follow Eusebius' advice, and promote the idea of multiple concurrent dynasties. The reason there were so many kings, was because there were multiple kings ruling at the same time. In this theory, there would have been different kings ruling from different capitals, at the same time.

The advocates of this new short timeline decided that some of the dynasties in the Old and Middle Kingdoms were just provincial governors that Manetho had intentionally added to his king lists to make the Egyptian Civilization seem older than it was. One of the leading promoters of this idea in the mid-1800s was Chevalier Bunsen, a German scholar and diplomat. Using the multiple concurrent dynastic approach Bunsen calculated the foundation of Egypt as being in 3643 BC, after God made the world, but before He destroyed it with the Great Deluge. Proponents of this theory believed that the Old Kingdom was a pre-flood civilization, while the Middle and New Kingdoms were post-flood. This first version of the short-timeline was disproved by Auguste Mariette, who pointed out that dynasties often erected monuments in cities other than their capitals, including the capitals from other dynasties. If they were competing dynasties, this could not have happened. Additionally, the Turin and Abydos King Lists were discovered proving that Manetho had faithfully compiled a king list that matched what the New Kingdom era Egyptians had believed a thousand years before him. Egyptologists universally turned back to the long timeline.

Ancient Kingdoms and Dark Ages

The reason there are so many options when dating Egyptian history is due to its complexity. Ancient Egypt wasn't a kingdom that built a bunch of pyramids and was then conquered by the Greeks. What we today call Ancient Egypt was, in fact, a series of kingdoms that rose and fell in the Nile region over several thousand years. They are called the Old, Middle, and New Kingdoms by Egyptologists. Separating these kingdoms were dark ages, which Egyptologists call the First, Second, and Third Intermediate Periods. Following the Third Intermediate Period, or third Egyptian dark age, was the Late Period when Egypt attempted to rebuild for the fourth time, but then fell under the control of foreigners.

Followers of both the short and long timelines agreed when the New Kingdom was founded, and pretty much everything that happened afterward. The New Kingdom was founded approximately 1580 BC ULT (1549 BC CET) and is the Kingdom of Egypt referenced in the Tanakh (Bible's Old Testament), where the Israelites were apparently enslaved for some time. It is also the Egypt of Greek mythology, where Helen had apparently been during the Battle of Troy, according to Herodotus and later writers. This was also the Egypt that fought the Hittites for control of Canaan, and can, therefore, be found in Hittite, Assyrian, and Babylonian records from that period. Additionally, radiocarbon dating has firmly placed the beginning of the New Kingdom between

1570 and 1544 BC.[4] The dating of this kingdom is simply not in doubt, other than a few decades one way or the other.

The New Kingdom collapsed around 1102 BC ULT (1077 BC CET) primarily due to environmental factors. The dendro-timeline, which is the timeline of Earth's ecological history for the past few thousand years worked out by studying tree rings, shows that around 1160 to 1140 BC the world became dark for a couple of decades, and there was very little plant growth. This is believed to have been a major factor in the collapse of several civilizations in the following century. The period of darkness is believed to have been caused by the eruption of the Hekla 3 volcano in Iceland, which would have filled the atmosphere with ash, blocking sunlight. This is believed to be where the term 'dark age' is derived, as the Greek Dark Age began then, and recorded massive migrations and invasions at the onset. In the case of Egypt, there were additional droughts caused by low rainfalls in Ethiopia, which is the source of most of the Nile's water. The kingdom fractured and ultimately fell to invading armies from Libya to the west, Nubia to the south, and Assyria to the northeast.

[4] Christopher Bronk Ramsey, et al. (2010) "Radiocarbon-Based timeline for Dynastic Egypt," *Science*, Volume 328, Number 5985, Pages 1554-1557

Second Egyptian Dark Age

While there is a general agreement on what happened after the New Kingdom, there is a great deal of disagreement over what happened before. The reason for the disagreements over the pre-New Kingdom dates stem from the fact that there are gaps in the Egyptian records for the First and Second Egyptian Dark Ages. The third Egyptian dark age, also called the Greek Dark Age, lasted just over 400 years, while the Western Dark Age, from the Fall of Rome to the Renaissance lasted approximately 1000 years. It is the question of "How long were those dark ages?" that drives the debate over the age of Egypt.

The second Egyptian dark age saw the collapse of the Middle Kingdom, widespread famine, the invasion of Egypt by the Hyksos from the Middle East, and the invasion of Egypt by the Nubians from the south. This was followed by a period of time during which the country was divided under the rule of these two foreign peoples, and ultimately a series of wars in which the native Egyptians drove out the foreigners. It is generally agreed that the Second Egyptian Dark Age comprises the 13th through 17th Dynasties.

The exact reason for the collapse of the Middle Kingdom is unclear, however, what is known is that there was a prolonged famine, and the last pharaoh of the 12th Dynasty, Queen Sobekneferu, had no heirs. It is believed by some Egyptologists that the first pharaoh of the 13th Dynasty was Sobekneferu's nephew, however, there is no clear evidence of this. In fact, Egyptologists disagree over who the first pharaoh of the 13th Dynasty was, some stating Sekhemre Khutawy Sobekhotep I, and others stating Khutawyre Wegaf. The reason forth this disagreement is caused by the fact that there are multiple ancient incomplete and conflicting king lists for this dynasty. Nevertheless, whoever it was, the transition from Sobekneferu to this new pharaoh was peaceful, indicating that he was likely related to Sobekneferu.

The 13th Dynasty is usually described as an era of chaos and disorder. The dynasty was undoubtedly characterized by decline, with a large number of kings with short reigns and only a few references to them found in the ruins of Egypt. It is clear that they were not from the same family line, and some of them were born commoners. The true timeline of this dynasty is difficult to determine as there are few monuments dating from the period. Many of the kings' names are only known from odd fragmentary inscriptions.

During the 13th Dynasty the Egyptian economy faltered, and Egypt began withdrawing its armies from the southern fortresses built during the Middle Kingdom. These fortresses were deep in Nubian territory, which Egypt had been colonizing during the Middle Kingdom. As the Egyptian power waned during the second Egyptian dark age, Nubian power grew united under the rule of the Kingdom of Kush, and ultimately Nubia invaded and then occupied southern Egypt.

One of the primary ways that the CET and ULT differ is that the CET has multiple dynasties coexisting during the dark ages, while the ULT has them generally in sequence. The difference reflects how the 14th Dynasty is interpreted. In the CET, the 14th Dynasty is a regional kingdom that broke away from Egypt sometime in the 12th Dynasty and ruled the Nile Delta for somewhere between 75 and 155 years. In the ULT, the 14th Dynasty followed the 13th Dynasty and ruled all of Egypt.

The exact borders of the 14th Dynasty are not known due to the general scarcity of monuments left by this dynasty. Seals attributable to the 14th Dynasty have been found throughout Egypt, including territory that advocates of the CET claim were under the rule of the 13th Dynasty. Additionally, 14th Dynasty seals have been found as far south as Dongola, deep in Nubia, and as far north as Tel Kabri, deep in Canaan. This indicates that the 14th Dynasty still had extensive control of, or at least influence over, the territories of the Middle Kingdom, and strongly supports the ULT.

In the CET, the Nubian Kingdom of Kush invaded southern Egypt in the 13th and 14th Dynasties, which were happening concurrently, and then both dynasties were invaded by people from the northeast called the Hyksos. In the ULT, the 14th Dynasty, which followed the 13th Dynasty, was invaded by Kush to the south, and then the Hyksos to the northeast.

The origin and nature of the Hyksos are also unclear, what is known is that they invaded from the Middle East. The term 'Hyksos' derives from the Egyptian expression 'heqau khaswet' which translates as 'rulers of foreign lands,' and was in use for centuries before the so-called Hyksos invasion to refer to any foreign government. This invasion was historically described as violent, but after a century of excavations into second Egyptian dark age ruins, it is now believed to have been a peaceful migration. It is known that there was both famine and plague in Egypt at the time, and so these immigrants were probably settling in virtually empty towns.

According to the ancient Egyptians before occupying Egypt, the Hyksos had conquered the Amorites and Canaanites, which on the CET should have happened shortly before the invasion of Egypt circa 1674 BC. According to Assyriologists, using the Conventional Mesopotamian Timeline (CMT) this was during the reign of King Abi-eshuh of the First Babylonian Empire, and the reign of King Bazaya of the Old Assyrian Empire. Yet neither the Babylonians or Assyrians noticed an army of Semites, Hurrians, and Indo-Aryans sneaking through their territory, and conquering their trading partners: the Amorites and Canaanites, before launching an invasion of their greatest rival: Egypt.

On the ULT the Hyksos invasion of Egypt happened during the Babylonian Dark Age, and the Hyksos were the Mitanni. In the ULT the Hittite Empire sacked Babylon circa 3038 BC, and the Babylonian Empire was left in disarray. The Mittani-Aryan and Kassites from the Zagros Mountains migrated into Babylonia approximately 25 years later circa 3013 BC. This group was not unified at the time, comprising a confederation or horde. In either timeline, the early Kassite rule of Babylonia was poorly documented, and there are large gaps in the historical records for the Babylonian Dark Age. In the ULT a faction of Kassites and Indo-Aryans invaded and conquered the Amorites and Canaanites forming the Mitanni Kingdom shortly after occupying Babylonia. This so-called 'empire' was also a confederation throughout its existence, as proven by the Battle of Meggido, where Thutmose III's armies fought an alliance of 330 Mitanni princes supporting the city of Kadesh circa 1457 BC. After defeating the combined armies of the 330 Mitanni princes at Meggido, Thutmose III's army was able to launch an invasion of the Mittani Empire a few years later, capturing the king without facing any defending army.

Centuries after the occupation of Babylonia and the establishment of the Mitanni Kingdom, the Kassite-Mittani invaded Egypt in circa 2533 BC ULT, or, shortly after conquering the Amorites and Canaanites, the mysterious and sneaky Hyksos invaded Egypt in 1674 BC CET without the Babylonian or Assyrian empires noticing. Either way, the Hyksos formed the 15th Dynasty, which did for some period of time control all of Egypt north of Nubia. The following 16th Dynasty is hotly debated by Egyptologists, with some CET proponents stating it was a vassal kingdom of the 15th Dynasty, and other CET proponents claiming it was an independent kingdom, while in the ULT it was an Egyptianized-Hyksos dynasty that ruled northern Egypt after the 15th Dynasty. Very little is known of this dynasty, even the number of kings is debated.

One of the reasons for the lack of information regarding these dynasties is that an insurgent dynasty called the Abydos Dynasty rose up as an Egyptian nationalist faction that spent three decades driving the Hyksos out of Egypt, in the process vilifying them, and then destroying all references to them. The Abydos Dynasty and the 17th Dynasty they subsequently established would, however, lay the foundation of the New Kingdom that rose up around 1580 BC ULT (1549 BC CET).

The Abydos Dynasty was not listed by Manetho and so doesn't have a dynastic number until after they had driven the Hyksos from Egypt when they became the 17th Dynasty. The information we have on the Abydos Dynasty today is drawn entirely from Egyptology, however, it does not add any years to either timeline as the Abydos and Sixteenth Dynasties were definitely concurrent.

So, how long did the Second Egyptian Dark Age last? How long did the 13th through 17th dynasties last? The collapse of the Middle Kingdom, the invasion of the Nubians, the immigration of the Hyksos, the century-long Hyksos dynasty, the 30-year war to drive them out of Egypt, and reign of the 17th Dynasty that started the Egyptian economic recovery? According to the ULT: 1666 years, according to the CET: 206 years!

This situation was under heavy debate early in the 20th century when Sir W. M. Flinders Petrie summed it up:

> "Setting aside altogether for the present the details of the list of Manetho, let us look only to the monuments, and the Turin papyrus of kings, which was written with full materials concerning this age, with a long list of kings, and only two or three centuries later than the

period in question. On the monuments we have the names of 17 kings of the XIIIth dynasty. In the Turin papyrus there are the lengths of reigns of 9 kings, amounting to 67 years, or 7 years each on an average. If we apply this average length of reign to only the 17 kings whose reigns are proved by monuments, we must allow them 120 years ; leaving out of account entirely about 40 kings in the Turin papyrus, as being not yet known on monuments. Of the Hyksos kings we know of the monuments of three certainly ; and without here adopting the long reigns stated by Manetho, we must yet allow at least 30 years for these kings. And in the XVIIth dynasty there are at least the reigns of Karnes and Sekhent nebra, which cover probably 10 years. Hence for those kings whose actual contemporary monuments are known there is required:

XIIIth dynasty . . 120 years

Hyksos at least 30 [years]

XVIIth dynasty . . 10 [years]

160 [years]

This leaves us but 46 years, out of the 206 years, to contain 120 kings named by the Turin papyrus, and all the Hyksos conquest and domination, excepting 30 years named above.

This is apparently an impossible state of affairs ; and those who advocate this shorter interval are even compelled to throw over the Turin papyrus altogether, and to say that within two or three centuries of the events an entirely false account of the period was adopted as the state history of the Egyptians."[5]

---

[5] W. M. Flinders Petrie (1906) *Researches In Sinai*, Pages 166-167

Manetho calculated the age of Egypt by adding together the number of years each pharaoh ruled, believing they ruled one after another and skipped the Abydos dynasty as they were concurrent with the 16th Dynasty. Conversely, the proponents of the CET have multiple dynasties ruling at the same time, and even have the 15th Dynasty starting before the 14th Dynasty, and the 12th Dynasty starting before the 13th Dynasty in order to make the numbers fit. As most of the records from the period were destroyed by the 17th and 18th Dynasties, there is little evidence one way or the other.

There is however the question of the collapse of the Middle Kingdom, which was caused by famine. If the CET is correct then the collapse happened around 1803 BC, a time that shows no evidence of significant climatic issues in the geologic records. If the ULT is correct, this happened around 3246 BC, in a period referred to as the Great Shock of 3250 BC. This is the point in time that the world's climate changed significantly into a neo-glacial period that lasted until around 1500 BC. There are a number of pieces of evidence supporting the existence of this Great Shock of 3250 BC.

During this time the world's weather became stormier, and there was far more rain, which would have caused significant flooding along the Nile, and in the Fayum, as well as along other rivers throughout the world.[6] The GISP2 ice core samples from

---

[6] Lisa L. Ely, et al. (October 15, 1993) "A 5000-Year Record of Extreme Floods and Climate Change in the Southwestern United States," *Science*, New Series, Volume 262, Number 5132, Pages 410-412

Greenland show there was a spike in atmospheric sulfate at 3250 BC, believed to have been from an increasing number of polynyas in the Arctic, caused by an expansion of oceanic surface ice.[7] The GRIP ice core sample from Greenland shows the 3250 BC point as being at a low point in atmospheric methane, followed by a rapid increase over the next 200 years, which is attributed to an abrupt increase in global wetlands.[8] Ice core samples from the Huascaran glacier in Peru, show an abrupt cooling at about 3250 BC.[9]

So there are two options:

1) the CET which states the Middle Kingdom collapsed around 1803 BC, for unknown reasons. It was followed by multiple concurrent dynasties, that fought multiple wars against foreign powers, ultimately being occupied, and then fought another war for their independence, all of which happened in around 200 years.

2) the ULT which states the Middle Kingdom collapsed around 3246 BC during the global climatic change called the Great Shock of 3250 BC. It was followed by a series of dynasties that fought a series of losing wars against invaders, ultimately being occupied, and then fought a war for their independence, which took place over 1600 years.

---

[7] G. A. Zielinski, et al. (1994) *Nature*, Volume 264, Page 948

[8] T. Blunier, et al. (1995) *Nature*, Volume 374, Page 47

[9] L. G. Thompson, et al. (July 7, 1995) "Late Glacial Stage and Holocene Tropical IceCore Records from Huascaran, Peru," *Science*, Volume 269, Pages 46-50.

Egyptian Middle Kingdom

To consider the collapse of the Middle Kingdom, and how long the second Egyptian dark age lasted one needs to consider the nature of the Middle Kingdom, as well as the differences between the Middle Kingdom and the New Kingdom. The Middle Kingdom emerged from the First Egyptian Dark Age and built on the ruins of the Old Kingdom. The Middle Kingdom lasted around 350 years, spanning the 11th and 12th dynasties. Both the ULT and CET generally agree about the length of the Middle Kingdom's history. The Middle Kingdom was also highly militant occupying most of Nubia to the south, and parts of Canaan to the northeast.

The major building projects of the Middle Kingdom were focused on waterworks and unlike the Old Kingdom, they only built small pyramids. This kingdom created the 15 km long Great Canal in the Bahr Yussef, that ran from the Nile to the Fayum. The Fayum is a natural depression west of Giza that was filled with water after the Grand Canal opened, creating Lake Moeris which was comparable in size to Lake Ontario in North America. The land around Lake Moeris became the breadbasket of Egypt and would remain so throughout the rest of Egyptian history until the Greek Period.

The Egyptians of the Middle and New Kingdoms did not speak the same language, although the languages were similar, like comparing ancient Latin to modern Italian. The language of the Middle Kingdom is called Middle-Egyptian by Egyptologists, while the language of the New Kingdom and later periods is called Late-Egyptian. Middle-Egyptian was standardized during the 11th dynasty and then evolved into Late-Egyptian during the second Egyptian dark age, which was ultimately standardized during the 18th Dynasty. Middle-Egyptian continued to be used as a literary language alongside Late-Egyptian much as Latin continues to be used as a clerical and academic language alongside Italian and other modern languages. Nevertheless, during the 400-year-long third Egyptian dark age the language did not change noticeably, yet according to CET proponents during the 200-year-long second Egyptian dark age, the language went through significant changes. This is clear evidence supporting the ULT, as significant changes, such as those that allowed Latin to morph into Italian take long periods of time.

The dominant religion of the Middle Kingdom was the Cult of Amen, who had been part of the Hermopolitan Ogdoad during the Old Kingdom. During the second Egyptian dark age, the Cult of Amen merged with the Cult of Ra, becoming the Cult of Amen-Ra, which was generally the dominant cult throughout the New Kingdom. Amen was originally a mystery god whose name meant something like 'the invisible one,' while Ra was the Sun-god by the beginning of the second Egyptian dark age, after originally being a creator god in the Old Kingdom.

Another major development during the second Egyptian dark age was the development of the Book of the Dead. During the Middle Kingdom, the dominant religious texts were the Coffin Texts, which was a precursor to the *Book of the Dead*. The focus of the Coffin Texts was Osiris, and the spirit's journey to the Duat, or afterlife, while the later *Book of the*

Dead was focused on Osiris' death, and the struggle of his son Horus against his brother Set.

Egyptologists believe the *Book of the Dead* developed as a propaganda piece used by nationalists to help turn the people against the Hyksos 16th Dynasty whose kings were associated with the god Set. According to the CET, this new religious text developed over a thirty year period between 1580 to 1549 BC. This is a very short period for a new religion to develop and be taught to the common people that needed to be turned against the Hyksos. Meanwhile, the ULT allows hundreds of years for the development of this religion and its adoption by the populous, which seems more likely given the centuries that Christianity and Buddhism took to develop and become adopted by a significant portion of the population.

The development of the Cult of Amen during the Middle Kingdom either dates to 2061 to 1803 BC CET or 3502 to 3246 BC ULT. The Cult of Amen included the blue-skinned god Amen as part of the Theban Triad. This triad included his wife Mut, which meant 'mother,' and his son Khonsu, which meant 'traveler.' While Amen was depicted as blue-skinned, Mut was depicted as light-skinned, and Khonsu was depicted as brown-skinned.

The Theban Triad is very iconically similar to the Puri Triad from India, which includes the blue-skinned Krishna, the brown-skinned Subhadra, and the light-skinned Balarama. The life of Krishna is dated by various ancient Indian sources to between approximately 3227 to 3102 BC, during the Harap-

41

pan Civilization. According to the Mahabharata, Krishna died in a fortress on an island off the coast of India near the city of Dwarka. After he died the fortress was reported to have sunk into the sea, which is believed by Hindus to have happened in 3102 BC. The remains of a large sunken structure have been discovered in waters off the coast of Dwarka, which does at least make the traditional dating for Krishna's life plausible. If the Puri Triad dates to around 3227 to 3102 BC, and the two triads have a common source, it seems far more likely the Theban Triad dates to sometime around 3502 to 3246 BC than sometime around 1500 years later.

While this might seem like a non-sequitur, the Egyptians were trading with the Harappans at the time, and the ULT considers not only the evidence in Egypt, but also their trading partners. The timeline of the Sumerian and Harappan Civilizations are both impacted by the use of the ULT in Egypt, as both cultures not only can, but must exist earlier than currently documented by Assyriologists and Indologists. Fortunately both cultures have both ruins and written records of earlier periods of their own civilizations, which no longer need to be dismissed as fiction. In the case of the Harappan Civilization, there are the Ramayana, Mahabharata, and other ancient Indian epics which tell of an ancient civilization that once existed in South Asia. A civilization which was described as being in the same lands as the Harappan civilization, and at the same time. As the Harappans were actively trading with the Sumerians prior to going into decline circa 3250 BC, and both cultures were trading with the Egyptians, it seems illogical to assume that the two iconically identical triads formed independently.

First Egyptian Dark Age

Before the Middle Kingdom, was the dark age known as the First Intermediate Period. Again this period of time is subject to a great deal of debate as again the written records of the time period are fragmentary. This time period spans the 7th through 10th Dynasties, which either took around 125 years according to the CET or around 500 years according to the ULT. In the CET, the first Egyptian dark age took place between approximately 2181 and 2040 BC, while in the ULT it took place between approximately 4003 and 3502 BC.

If the Old Kingdom collapsed around 2181 BC, there are no clear reasons why it collapsed. Several reasons are listed by Egyptologists, primarily focused on the long reign of Pepi II, the last major pharaoh of the 6th Dynasty. Pepi II ruled for over seven decades, which according to Egyptologists caused the collapse of the Old Kingdom because he outlived his immediate successors. This long-lived king apparently caused the destabilization of the kingdom, unlike other long-lived monarchs throughout human history, which generally created stability.

Another theory which has been proposed is the so-called 4.2 Kiloyear Event. This event is theorized to have happened, largely based on the fact that Egypt supposedly collapsed at this time. The Akkadian civilization also collapsed around this point, however, the dating of the Akkadian empire is also unclear as there were three dark ages after the fall of the Akkadian Empire, correlating to the Egyptian dark ages. The earliest clear correlations between the Mesopotamian civilizations and Egyptian civilizations date to the 13th Dynasty in the Middle Kingdom.

Unlike most environmental events throughout the past few thousand years, the so-called 4.2 Kiloyear Event is not known from traditional environmental indicators such as ice-core-samples. The 4.2 Kiloyear Event was theorized because there appears to have been a drying period at the end of the Old Kingdom, which CET proponents place around 2181 BC. Conversely, if the Old Kingdom collapsed around 4003 BC, it correlates to the 5.9 Kiloyear Event, which took place between 4200 and 3900 BC. The 5.9 Kiloyear Event is known from multiple physical sources, and ties into the rapid drying in Tadrart Acacus of southwestern Libya.

The first Egyptian dark age is clearly a time of chaos, and virtually nothing is known of the 7th Dynasty. Many Egyptologists believe the dynasty may not have happened at all. The source for the dynasty is Manetho's Aegyptiaca, which unfortunately no longer exists, and the quotes of Aegyptiaca do not agree on what the 7th Dynasty was. Africanus' quote from around 200 AD lists 70 kings in 70 days, while Eusebius' quote from around 300 AD lists 5 kings in 75 days. Whatever caused the collapse of the Old Kingdom seems to have been complete, leaving nothing but chaos in the aftermath.

The 8th Dynasty is generally accepted by Egyptologists and is also interpreted as a time of chaos by Egyptologists. Africanus' and Eusebius' quotes of Manetho also disagree, with Africanus quoting the 8th Dynasty as lasting 27 kings who reigned for 146 years, and Eusebius quoting 5 kings who reigned for 100 years. There is virtually no archaeological evidence for the Seventh or Eighth Dynasties, and as a result, modern Egyptologists only assign around 25 years for both dynasties, while the ULT accepts the idea that these dynasties took place over 100 to 150 years.

There is also very little archaeological evidence for the Ninth and Tenth Dynasties, however, Egyptologists do generally agree that the dynasties existed. The Turin King List from the New Kingdom listed 18 kings for the 9th Dynasty, although the names are lost. As there is little archaeological evidence, modern Egyptologists allow for the 18 kings to have reigned for only 30 years between 2160 and 2130 BC. This means that each king ruled an average of less than 2 years. As there is more evidence for the 10th Dynasty Egyptologists recognize 5 pharaohs who reigned for 90 years between 2130 and 2040 BC, which averages 18 years per king. Conversely, the ULT accepts 285 years for the two dynasties between 3787 and 3502 BC, which averages around 12 years per king.

Unfortunately, there is very little evidence remaining from the first Egyptian dark age, meaning that it is unlikely to be proven when exactly the period was. Nevertheless, the collapse of the Old Kingdom at the proven 5.9 Kiloyear Event makes more sense than at a hypothetical 4.2 Kiloyear event that lacks all paleo-climatological evidence. If the Old Kingdom ended around 2181 BC in the CET, then it would have been founded around 2686 BC. On the other hand, if the Old Kingdom ended around 4003

BC in the ULT, then it would have begun around 4945 BC.

Egyptian Old Kingdom

The Old Kingdom spanned the 3rd through 6th Dynasties and was the time when the ancient Egyptians are believed to have built the great pyramids, Sphinx, and ancient megalithic temples near the Sphinx. The Old Kingdom was preceded by the Early Dynastic era which covered the 1st and 2nd Dynasties. The Early Dynastic era is not clearly understood due to limited and conflicting information from the period. By the beginning of the Old Kingdom, enough information remains for us to have a relatively complete understanding of the next few centuries.

The first king of the Old Kingdom was Djoser of the 3rd Dynasty, who ordered the construction of the step pyramid in Saqqara, near Memphis. Like the later Middle and New Kingdoms, the Old Kingdom had a distinct form of Egyptian, which is now known as Old-Egyptian. Old-Egyptian was written similar to Middle-Egyptian, however, it was clearly a different spoken dialect. There were some minor differences between the hieroglyphs used in the Old Kingdom to those used in the Middle and New Kingdoms, however, they remained largely unchanged throughout Egyptian history until the adoption of the Coptic script during the Greek Era. Hieroglyphs themselves date back to the pre-Dynastic period, although pre-Dynastic Hieroglyphs are generally untranslatable, and the Archaic-Egyptian of the first two dynasties is scarce.

Throughout the Old, Middle, and New Kingdoms, the more common script used was the hieratic script, which is considered to be a simplified form of hieroglyphs. During the third Egyptian dark age, which coincides with the Greek dark age, the Egyptians developed the Demotic script, which seems to have been influenced by Aramaic, and was used alongside hieroglyphs until the Christian era, when the Greek-influenced Coptic script was developed.

The fact that the Old Kingdom had a different dialect of spoken Egyptian is extremely significant, as it seems highly unlikely that a new dialect would have developed and become dominant in the 125 years allotted by the CET, however, it is plausible in the 500 years allotted by the ULT. This is re-enforced by the fact that both dialects used the same written scripts, and there are no signs of invasions by foreigners.

The question of 'when was the Old Kingdom?' is essential to understanding the physical evidence found from that period, and the nature of the kingdom itself. Regardless of when it was, most Egyptologists agree that during the Old Kingdom all the large pyramids were built, the Sphinx was carved, and the megalithic temples were built. There have been consistent dissenters throughout the past two centuries regarding the Sphinx, megalithic temples, and Osireion, which some Egyptologists, as well as other researchers, believe might be from an earlier unknown period of civilization due to their unusual and unique construction techniques.

There are also those that believe the Great Pyramid of Khufu must have been built before the mastabas that surround it. The mastabas date to the 3rd Dynasty, whereas the Pyramid of Khufu is believed to have been built in the 4th Dynasty. Nevertheless, the accepted history has the Great Pyramids of Giza, and maybe the Sphinx and megalithic temples near the Sphinx built in the 4th Dynasty.

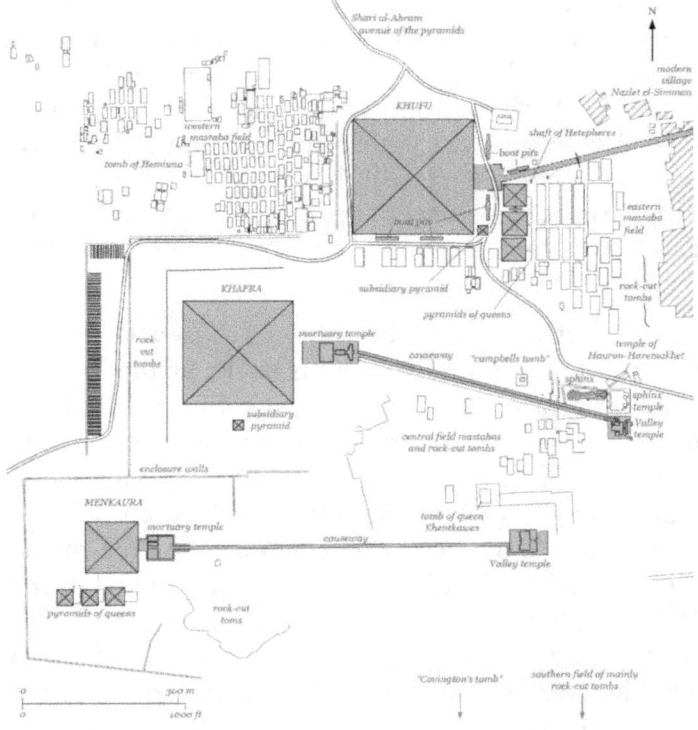

If this kingdom existed between 2686 and 2181 BC, as claimed in the CET it existed entirely within the dry period that began with the 5.9 Kiloyear Event. On the other hand, if the Old Kingdom existed between 4945 and 4003 BC, it existed during the African Humid Period and collapsed during the 5.9 Kiloyear Event.

The African Humid Period is well documented by samples taken from multiple dried lakes and rivers across the modern Sahara Desert. Between 14,000 and 4,000 BC the Sahara was a fertile land of rainforests and savannas like equatorial Africa is today. During this time the Nile would have received much higher water flow year-round than after the 5.9 Kiloyear Event, as not only were the Blue and White Nile Rivers receiving more in-flow, but the Yellow and Black Niles were still flowing year round. These other tributaries of the Nile, dried up during the 5.9 Kiloyear Event, becoming seasonal wadis, as they continue to be today.

Given that the Giza Plateau has causeways reaching out towards the Nile, with docks at the end for ships to unload their stone blocks, there must have been water present at the docks during the Old Kingdom. Furthermore, given that the Sphinx enclosure shows signs of significant water damage, it seems clear that there was water in the area of the Sphinx enclosure after the Sphinx was created. If the Old Kingdom existed between 2686 and 2181 BC, there is no explanation for this water. If the Old Kingdom existed between 4945 and 4003 BC, the source of the water is explained by the annual Nile river floods, which would have been much higher than they were after the 5.9 Kiloyear Event. This would also explain why the major construction efforts of the Middle Kingdom were geared towards water conservation and agricultural expansion. During the African Humid Period, rainwater and Nile overflow would have naturally collected in the Fayum depression forming a natural Lake Moeris, however, by the Middle Kingdom, the Grand Canal had to be dug connecting the depression to the lower level of the Nile.

If both kingdoms existed during the dry period after the 5.9 Kiloyear Event there is no explanation as to why the Middle Kingdom felt they needed so much more water than the Old Kingdom had apparently needed. Conversely, if the Middle Kingdom is what rebuilt after the 5.9 Kiloyear Event, their obsession with water is justified. The entire harbor area for Giza was altered by the kings of the Old Kingdom so they could get their ships to the plateau.

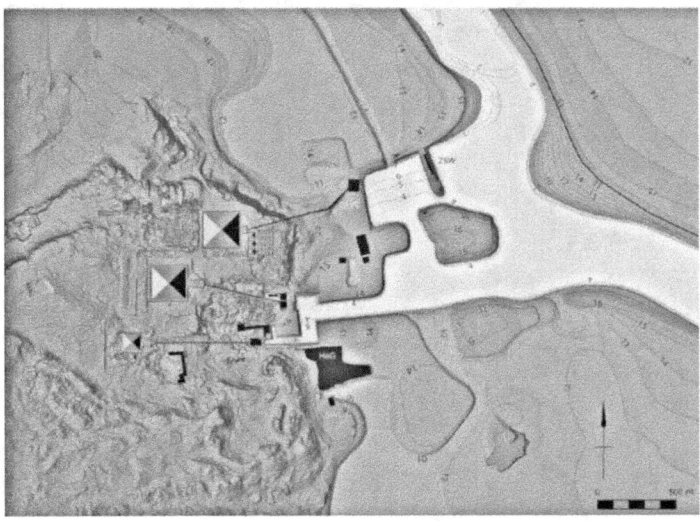

The Nile was clearly altered greatly during the Old Kingdom, however, the initial placement for the harbors for both Khafre and Menkure make much more sense on the higher water level of the Nile during the Humid African Period prior to 4000 BC.

Surely building longer causeways would have been easier than dredging out a thousand times as much mud to change the path of the Nile. Nevertheless, the Old Kingdom did dredge out the vast harbor area to maintain the existing dock area. The only logical explanation for this is that the Nile dropped drastically during the course of the Old Kingdom, which it would have if it was in the last few centuries of the African Humid Period. Evidence of this drastic drop between the 4th Dynasty when the Giza Pyramids were built, and the 6th Dynasty when the Old Kingdom ended, can be found right behind the Sphinx enclosure. The previous image shows the Nile during the Old Kingdom era circa 2686 to 2181 BC CET, and the next image is with the water level of the Old Kingdom in 4945 to 4003 BC ULT.

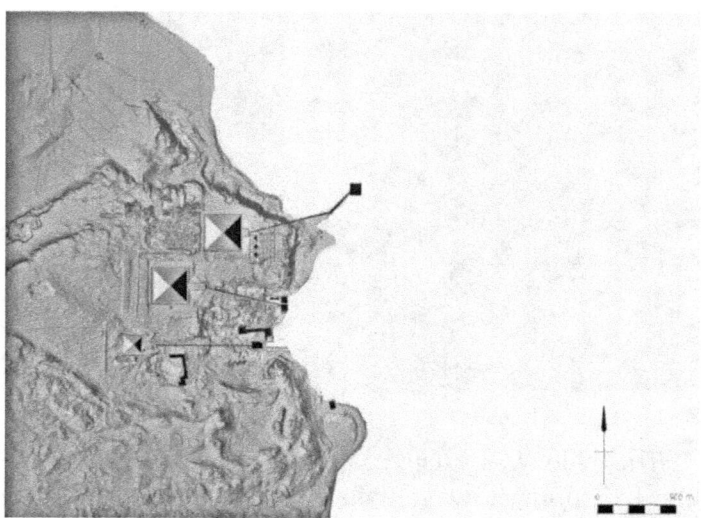

During the 6th Dynasty, the so-called Osiris Shaft was dug. This shaft started on the surface about halfway between the Sphinx and the Pyramid of Khafre, north of the causeway, which was partially taken apart in order to dig a well 30 meters (~90 feet) deep. The name Osiris Shaft, or Tomb of Osiris, is derived from the Egyptian Egyptologist Zahi Hawass obser- vation that the tomb at the bottom of the shaft seems iconically similar to the Osireion. It is also called Campbell's Tomb, named after the British Consul to Egypt at the time when it was rediscovered in 1830 AD by Howard Vyse and Giovanni Caviglia. Vyse and Caviglia had the sand cleared out to a depth of 30 meters, and removed a basalt sarcophagus that now resides at the British Museum. The next major excavation wasn't until 1933-34 by the Egyptian Egyptologist Selim Hassan who described it in An- tiquity in 1944:

> *"Upon the surface of the causeway they first built a platform in the shape of a mastaba, using stones taken from the ruins of the covered corridor of the causeway. In the centre of this superstructure they sank a shaft, which passed through the roof and floor of the subway running under the causeway to a depth of about 9.00 m. At the bottom of this shaft is a rectangular chamber, in the floor of the eastern side of which is another shaft. This descends about 14.00 m. and terminates in a spacious hall surrounded by seven burial-chambers, in each of which is a sarcophagus. Two of these sarcophagi, which are of basalt and are monolithic, are so enormous that at first we wondered if they contained the bodies of sacred bulls.*
>
> *In the eastern side of this hall is yet another shaft, about 10.00 m. deep, but unfortunately it*

is flooded. Through the clear water we can see that it ends in a colonnaded hall, also having side-chambers containing sarcophagi. We tried in vain to pump out the water, but it seems that a spring must have broken through the rock, for continual daily pumping over a period of four years was unable to reduce the water-level. I may add that I had this water analysed and finding it pure utilized it for drinking purposes"[10]

The water level that stopped Hassan's team had dropped enough by the 1990s that Zahi Hawass was able to excavate the lower level in 1999. Hawass was the first to associate the tomb at the bottom of the shaft with the description by Herodotus in The Histories circa 450 BC of the tomb of Khufu. Herodotus' description of the Tomb of Khufu was generally considered fiction by Egyptologists before Hawass noted the similarities. Hawass team also recovered pottery fragments at the lowest level dating to the 6th Dynasty, the last dynasty of the Old Kingdom, although also noted the burial chambers were added later during the Late Period. Presumably, the tomb was open circa 450 BC if Herodotus was able to describe it. Hawass' description of the Tomb of Osiris at the bottom of the shaft was published in 2007 on his blog at drhawass.com:

"The channel surrounding the emplacement in the lowest level seems to have been deliberately designed so that groundwater would fill it, making the emplacement in the centre into a sort of island. This configuration could represent the primeval waters of Nun, which covered the world at the time of creation,

---

[10] Selim Hassan (1944) "Excavations at Giza," *Antiquity*, Volume 18, Issue 70

with the island in the center representing the first mound of earth to emerge. The water further symbolizes the connection of Osiris to fertility and rebirth. The emplacement with a large sarcophagus in the centre and a pillar at each corner (perhaps representing the four sacred legs of the god as described in later texts) is very similar to the configuration of the Osireion of Seti I at Abydos

We were surprised to find that there was also some red polished pottery with traces of white paint, which probably dates to the 6th Dynasty. the earliest artefacts found inside date to Dynasty 6.

I believe that the Osiris Shaft is what the Greek author Herodotus, the "father of history," was talking about when he said that Khufu was buried on an island in an underground chamber, located in the shadow of the Great Pyramid and fed by a canal from the Nile."

The fact that the water level dropped by up to 30 meters between the 4th Dynasty and the 6th Dynasty is further proof that the CET is impossible, as a significant drop of the Nile level during the second millennium BC did not happen. If it had, the Nile at Giza would have been significantly below the sea level of the Mediterranean. This drop could only have happened at an earlier point when the African Humid Period was ending, circa 4000 BC.

The dropping water levels of the Nile at the end of the 4th Dynasty also explains the mysterious death of the god Horus the Elder. Before the late-4th dynasty, Horus the Elder was one of the preeminent gods of Egypt. He was the husband of Isis, and father of the four winds, who helped him ascend into the

sky each morning in his role as sun god. His importance was so established, that burial chambers included ladder icons representing his accension from
the underworld each morning. Yet, by the end of the
4th dynasty, he had disappeared. Isis was now mar-
ried to Osiris, the major sun god was Ra, and the
dominant sky god was Sah, the asterism that encom-
passed the later constellations Orion and Lupus.

Horus the Elder was essentially forgotten until
the ancient Greek historians rediscovered him thousands of years later. Modern Egyptologists have rediscovered more about this once important god who
vanished in the 4th dynasty, however, his death remains a mystery. In the later New Kingdom stories
about Osiris and Isis, Osiris was killed by Set, however, Isis later impregnated herself with Osiris' severed penis, and gave birth to Horus the Younger.
This suggests that Set may have originally killed Horus the Elder, however, Old Kingdom literature de-
picts them as allies. Nevertheless, by the New Kingdom, Sah was no longer associated with the stars of
Orion, Osiris was, and the Egyptians viewed the
stars the Greeks interpreted as Orion's sword, as
Osiris severed penis. This suggests the story about
Isis impregnating herself with Osiris' severed penis,
dates to after Osiris became associated with the stars
of Orion. This association appears to have originated
during the Middle Kingdom, and certainly existed
before the Hyksos were driven from Egypt during
the second Egyptian dark age.

While Osiris and Sah were not the same god, they
were both associated with the stars of Orion, and
were replacements for Horus the Elder in the late-

4th dynasty. By the Middle Kingdom, Sah was no longer a major god, yet in the late Old kingdom, he had been called the 'father of the gods.' Likewise, Isis had become associated with Sopdet, Sah's wife, who represented the star Sirius. Horus the Elder's replacement by gods associated with marking the passage of time, Sah, who ruled the night sky, Sopdet, who represented Sirius and was believed to predict the Nile floods each year, and their son Sopdu, who represented the planet Venus, suggests that there was a problem with the older calendar the Egyptians had been using. Venus was used to reset calendars every eight years by many ancient cultures, including the Sumerians and Mayans, due to the synchronicity of the orbits of Venus and Earth around the Sun, which results in Venus appearing in the same place in the sky every eight years.

Early Old Kingdom records of Horus the Elder, represented either as a falcon, or as what the Greeks would later dub the hieracosphinx, a falcon-headed-sphinx. This is most likely what the sphinx was before King Khafre re-carved the face, replacing it with his own. Egyptologist Hawass' discovery that the Giza Plateau was known as the Horizon of Horus during the era, confirms that the plateau was associated with Horus the elder before his death, although the association disappeared when he died. Khafre's re-carving his own face on the sphinx proves the god was dead to the Egyptians before the end of the 4th dynasty.

The sphinx was carved so that when viewing the sphinx head on, the sun sets over its right shoulder each equinox, both in March and September, and no other time of the year. This indicates that it was built for predicting the season changes, and sometime before the permanent water drop in the Nile around 6000 years ago.

A statue of a hieracosphinx from the New Kingdom era, currently at the British Museum.

Since the Nile levels dropped, the Heliacal rising of Sirius would have been far more pertinent than the middle of the dry season and the middle of the wet season, which is what the sphinx is positioned to indicate. Once the rains stopped, and the Nile dropped, the seasonal flooding which happened around 10 days after the summer solstice was far more important, and Sirius rose with the sun a few days before the flooding started each season. This again supports the ULT over the CET, but also supports the Inventory Stele discovered in 1857, which claimed that Khufu found the sphinx and ordered its repair. As Khufu lived before Khafre, this was once viewed as evidence that the sphinx was older than Khafre, however, the stele's dialect is Late Egyptian, suggesting it was either a copy of an older stele, or an outright fiction, and therefore, until an older copy is discovered, it is not considered indisputable evidence.

Nevertheless, Khafre did destroy the face of Horus when he put his face on the sphinx. A bust of Khafre has been discovered that is virtually identical to the sphinx's face. Additionally, the Giza Plateau was called the Horizon of Horus, and the Horus of the era was depicted as a falcon-headed lion. Therefore, it is highly probable that the Inventory Stele is correct, and Khufu ordered the rebuilding of the sphinx. However, something then took place that made the Egyptians turn against Horus the Elder sometime during the reign of Khafre. In the ULT, the cause is the Nile dropping 30 meters, and Khafre being unable to build the much larger pyramid he had planned.

Based on the area that was leveled off around the pyramid, it's clear that the pyramid was supposed to have been much larger than the pyramid of Khufu. The Pyramid of Khafre as it was built, has a base length of 215.25 meters[11] per side, however the area leveled for construction was approximately 245 meters long per side. The idea that the pyramid is significantly smaller than intended, allowed Giovanni Belzoni to locate the original entrance in 1818. He calculated where the entrance should have been on the larger pyramid and found the entrance approxi-

[11] Miroslav Verner (2001). *The Pyramids: The Mystery, Culture and Science of Egypt's Great Monuments.* Page 463.

mately 14 meters off of the center. This means that the original design was supposed to have a base length of approximately 245 meters, in comparison to the pyramid of Khufu's 230 meters. It was also being built on a section of the plateau that was 10 meters higher than where Khufu's pyramid stands, meaning if both pyramids were built at the same slope, it should have stood around 15 meters taller than Khufu's pyramid. However, as the entrance was built according to the original design, the design was obviously changed part way through construction, and therefore the steeper slope must have been part of the original design. Unlike Khufu's pyramid, which has a slope of 51°50',[12] the Pyramid of Khafre has a slope of 53°10'.[13] This steeper slope, and higher base, allows the Khafre's pyramid to rise around 10 meters higher into the sky than Khufu's even though is it a less massive pyramid. The original pyramid design appears to have been around 155.4 meters high, on a base 10 meters higher than Khufu's pyramid, and therefore would have stood around 20 meters taller than Khufu's pyramid.

Clearly, something catastrophic must have happened, to change the design part way through construction. The well of Osiris, built directly into the causeway, and descending for 30 meters, indicates that the Egyptians were desperate for drinking water on the causeway. It has several levels, which were later used as burial chambers in the 6th dynasty, however, clearly began as a well. The well has to have been built after the causeway, but during the

---

[12] Mark Lehner (2008). *The Complete Pyramids*. Page 108.
[13] Mark Lehner (2008). *The Complete Pyramids*. Page 17.

building of the pyramid, which indicates the water level fell 30 meters during the construction of Khafre's pyramid. This appears to be the cause of the pyramid being down scaled, and why Khafre was so enraged at Horus that he desecrated the god's face. However, it leaves the question of when the sphinx was originally built unanswered.

Foundation of Egypt

The 1st and 2nd Dynasties are very poorly understood, as Egyptologists cannot seem to find anything dating to the right time. This is dismissed as being due to the Early Dynastic period being very long ago, and very, very chaotic. Both those points are valid, however, in the CET the 1st Dynasty began circa 3100 BC, yet we've uncovered the ruins of cities dating back to 5000 to 5300 BC that seem fairly intact, so where are the early dynastic cities? In 2015, the remains of an unknown village were discovered in the Nile delta's Dakahlia governorate. As there was nothing that associated the village with any specific dynasty, carbon-dating was used to date the village, which showed it was approximately 7000 years old.[14] In 2016 another unknown village was found, this one in the vicinity of Abydos, and dated to around 5,316 BC using carbon dating. This 7300-year-old village was described by Egyptian archaeologist as:

> "The size of the graves discovered in the cemetery is larger in some instances than royal graves in Abydos dating back to the 1st Dynasty, which proves the importance of the people buried there and their high social standing during this early era of ancient Egyptian history."[15]

These discoveries essentially prove the existence of dynastic Egypt at approximately 5300 to 5000 BC, however, are not interpreted that way by Egyptolo-

---

[14] Lauren Said-Moorhouse (September 3, 2018) "Archaeologists unearth village in Egypt older than the pharaohs," *CNN.com*

[15] Reuters in Cairo (November 23, 2016) "Egypt unearths 7,000-year-old lost city," *The Guardian*

gists, who claim they are pre-dynastic. If Egyptologists accepted the ULT, the village found in the vicinity of Abydos would no doubt be accepted as the lost town of Thinis, where King Menes, also called Narmer, was from. Unfortunately, they cannot accept the ULT without admitting they've been wrong about the Egyptian timeline for the past century, so, they will likely never find Thinis, and they'll need to make up a new name for the village discovered in 2016. They'll also need to make up some more fiction explaining who these people were, who built exactly like the 1st Dynasty people in the Abydos region, and coincidentally lived in the Abydos region, but a couple of thousand years earlier.

Christian Timeline

So if the ULT fits the geological and paleoclimatological evidence far better than the CET, why has the CET become ubiquitous in Egyptology? In a word: Christianity.

Egyptologists were divided into two camps during the late-1800s, some supporting the long timeline, and some supporting the short timeline. The long timeline proponents based their views of Egyptian history on the ancient records of Egypt, while the short timeline proponents based their view of Egyptian history on the version of the Bible they were using at the time. The pattern was identical for Iraqi, Indian, and Chinese history, where the dates of the ancient Mesopotamian, Harappan, and the early Chinese civilizations were all simply moved to after the Great Flood.

The Great Flood is a story from Jewish folklore in which a massive global flood was once sent by one of the ancient Jewish gods to massacre all of humanity and some rebellious angels that were living on the planet at that time, along with a group of giants the angels had made by impregnating human women. There are dozens of known versions and variations of the story found in the early Christian, Jewish, Gnostic, and Mandaeism texts, however, one was adopted into the Christian Bible, and so Christian fundamentalists need for all of history to conform to the Biblical timeline, or accept that the writers of the Bible weren't omniscient. This rewriting of history across the world was so complete that even the current Chinese culture accepts the dating for the life of the Yellow Emperor at around 2,700 to

2,600 BC, a date invented by the Jesuit missionary Martino Martini in the 1600s. The fact is, China does have ancient records that predate the Jesuit mission to China, and which places the life of the Yellow Emperor approximately 6,200 to 6,100 BC, but they are ignored by the modern Chinese. In India and Pakistan, ruins have been excavated that are clearly part of the Harappan Civilization, yet date to 7000 BC, which Indian archaeologists recognize as part of a long term civilization. Western archaeologists ignore the ruins entirely, leaving the established date for the Harappan Civilization at 3300 to 1300 BC, after God made the world.

Ironically, almost all western scholars reject the creation and flood myths entirely, yet cling to the dating established by the earlier generations of historians and archaeologists, who insisted on dating ancient civilizations according to the biblical timeline. The shift to the CET that is so ubiquitous today, began with James Henry Breasted in the early 1900s. Brested is widely considered the father of American Egyptology having been the first American to obtain a Ph.D. in Egyptology, which he had earned from the University of Berlin in 1894. Shortly after receiving his Ph.D., he joined the faculty at the University of Chicago, where in 1901 he became director of the Haskell Oriental Museum, and in 1905 was promoted to full professor, holding the first chair in Egyptology and Oriental History in the United States.

Between 1899 to 1908 Brested conducted multiple fieldwork expeditions to Egypt, which established his reputation. He also published numerous articles and monographs, including his *History of Egypt from the Earliest Times Down to the Persian Conquest.* That he was a leading Egyptologist in his day is not doubted, however, modern Egyptologists generally ignore the fact that he was also a Christian fundamentalist. Brested began his post-secondary education at North-Western College, now known as North Central College, which was then, and continues to be affiliated with the United Methodist Church. From there he went on to attend the Chicago Theological Seminary which is a Christian ecumenical American seminary located in Chicago and was at the time affiliated with the United Church of Christ. Brested had been working on becoming a congregational minister, however, found his faith shaken by the idea that the biblical timeline might not be accurate.[16] Ultimately he transferred to Yale, where he received his master's degree before continuing on to the University of Berlin.

While he had obviously been educated in the then ubiquitous long timeline, he ultimately reformulated the then discredited short timeline, claiming the 1st Dynasty of Egypt was founded circa 3400 BC. While he did not mention the Biblical creation and great flood narratives, it is worth noting that his new dating places the Old Kingdom back where the earlier short timeline proponents placed it, before the flood, but after the creation of the world. This idea is not new, nor invented by Christians, in fact, Muslims scholars came to the same conclusions centuries earlier.

---

[16] Ludlow Bull, et al. (1936) "James Henry Breasted 1865-1935," *Journal of the American Oriental Society*, Volume 56, Pages 113-120

Islamic Timeline

Medieval Muslims believed that the Islamic prophet Idris was the Israelite patriarch Enoch, who lived before Noah's flood. The prophet Idris founded Egypt after leaving Babylon because the people there were being bad Muslims. This is a chronologically confusing sentence, however, it is consistent with medieval Islamic teachings, which some Muslims continue to believe today. The prophet Idris was also believed by some early Islamic scholars to be Hermes Trismegistus, who was the builder of the Great Pyramid of Khufu (Cheops) in Hermetic thought, while his brother Agathodaemon was the builder of the Pyramid of Khafre (Chephren) a thousand years earlier. This belief was documented by Al-Maqrizi around 1200 AD:

> "One of these pyramids is the tomb of A'adimun (also called Agathodaemon) and the other of Hermes. Between these two figures there are nearly a thousand years, A'adimun being the older of the two. The inhabitants of Egypt, that is to say the Copts, argue that these two characters were two prophets who appeared before the coming of Christianity."

Around a century earlier the Islamic scholar Al-Shahrastani wrote in the *Kitab al–Milal wa al-Nihal* that:

> "They say that Ads-imun and Hermes, were Seth and Enoch respectively."

To a medieval Muslim, this would mean that the Pyramids pre-dated the flood, as both the Islamic prophets Seth and Idris (Enoch) were prophets from before the time of Nuh (Noah). These Islamic prophets are also considered the Jewish and Christian pre-flood patriarchs Seth and Enoch, and the Gnostic enlighted beings Agathodaemon and Hermes Trismegistus, which lived before the flood. Naturally, Brested didn't mention any of this, as other historians and archaeologists would have thought him quite mad.

Although modern Egyptologists like to ignore the para-biblical timeline proposed by Brested or claim it is simply coincidence, it is a very strange coincidence that he placed the first Egyptian dark age at the time of the Great Flood. According to the then accepted translations of the Bible, the Great Flood happened in 2348 BC, while in Brested's short timeline the first Egyptian dark age happened between 2475 and 2160 BC.

This 'coincidence' did make Egyptian 'history' more palatable to Christians, who at the time dominated American and European politics and controlled the amount of money flowing into Egyptological research. Brested and those that followed his CET received far more funding than the heretics trying to disprove the correctness of the Holy Bible, and therefore Brested's CET slowly became dominant over the following decades.

The Even More Christian Timeline

In 1995, an even more Christian timeline was proposed by self-declared agnostic David Rohl in his work *A Test of Time: The Bible - from Myth to History*. Rohl's goal was to synchronize the Egyptian timeline with the Biblical timeline, an odd thing for an agnostic to do. One would expect an agnostic to try to synchronize the Biblical timeline with the Egyptian timeline, not the opposite, if an agnostic bothered to look into it at all.

In order to synchronize the Egyptian timeline to the Biblical timeline, Rohl proposes removing another 350 years from the CET, placing the foundation of the 1st Dynasty in 2770 BC. Rohl's proposed changes focus on the third Egyptian dark age, which Rohl wants to synchronize with the Tanakh. In the current version of the Egyptian Timeline, the Biblical King Shihsaq of Egypt is identified with King Shoshenq I, however, Rohl has suggested changing this to King Ramesses II, who lived hundreds of years earlier. In order to compress the timeline, Rohl has proposed that the 21st and 22nd Dynasty were contemporary.

This even more Christian timeline forces the Aegean and Mesopotamian timelines to be even more compressed than they already are. This means that the Mediterranean and Mesopotamian Iron Age would have started in the 800s BC, almost 1000 years after the Indian Iron Age, and 700 years after the Yaz Iron Age in Central Asia. This timeline is generally rejected by Egyptologists, however, there is a growing number of Egyptologists seriously considering it.

Carbon Dating

Of course, we are no longer living in that age, so what about modern scientific dating systems? Surely the Egyptologists have used carbon dating to prove when these kingdoms existed. Well, yes they have, and no they haven't. As the land of Egypt has been occupied for thousands of years, and only biologic materials can be carbon dated, and biological materials don't generally survive the passage of time, the situation is murky.

Early carbon dating tests showed the Old Kingdom to be thousands of years older than Egyptologists said it was,[17] so the Egyptologists rejected the science. More recent radiocarbon studies are very close to what the Egyptologists state using the CET, however, these results are found by systematically ignoring any results that deviate from the CET by more than one thousand years. Therefore the tests cannot prove that the Old Kingdom is 2400 years older than the CET demands because those results are systematically excluded.

The way these carbon dating tests are shaped by the CET and end up confirming the CET is simple to demonstrate. If the Old Kingdom was founded around 7500 years ago when the ULT indicates, there would have still been people living in Egypt around 5100 years ago when the CET indicates. In order to conduct tests scientists need pieces of biological artifacts from the time period they want to test, which they have to get from Egyptologists, who state when they believe the artifacts date from. This

---

[17] Robert M. Schoch (2003) *Voyages of the Pyramid Builders*

means that the scientists now already have a date that their tests need to correlate to, which means that the outcome shaping has already begun.

Egyptologists have always rejected carbon dating results that deviate greatly from the CET using one of several reasons. If the artifact isn't something that can be definitively dated to a specific dynasty, perhaps by an inscription on it, then the results can be dismissed by claiming the artifact was sent in error and must date from a different dynasty, or is predynastic. As carbon dating destroys the object tested, most artifacts sent to scientists are unimportant pieces of debris that don't include inscriptions. On the other hand, if the artifact can be positively linked to a specific dynasty yet the carbon dating is off by centuries or millennia, Egyptologists either claim the test was faulty or simply ignore the test results entirely.

There is of course also the scientific rebuttal of carbon dating for ancient times which some Egyptologists engaged in if pushed to explain away a carbon-date. The way carbon dating works is by comparing the amount of carbon to carbon-14 in an object. Carbon is found in three forms on Earth, carbon-12, carbon-13, and carbon-14, and while carbon-12 and carbon-13 are both stable and relatively common, carbon 14 is both unstable and rare. Carbon-14 is a radioisotope with a half-life of 5,730±40 years. This means that it is possible to figure out how long an organism has been dead by comparing the amount of carbon to carbon-14 in the body. The longer the organism has been dead, the less carbon-14 it will have, and therefore a calculation of the estimated time of death can be made. At least in the-ory.

In fact, the carbon-dating method depends on knowing how much carbon the organism was exposed to while alive, and what percentage of that carbon was carbon-14. If the amount of carbon in the atmosphere was stable, and if there were no new sources of carbon-14 being introduced, then the method would work exactly as envisioned, however, neither of those conditions are met on Earth. Every time a major volcanic eruption occurs, a massive quantity of carbon is spewed into the atmosphere. This carbon is believed to be almost entirely carbon-12, meaning that the percentage of carbon-14 in an organism that died after the eruption would be skewed by the extra carbon-12, and the organism may appear to had died decades earlier than a creature that died shortly before the eruption.

An additional variable is added when more carbon-14 is introduced to the environment. Carbon-12 and carbon-13 are converted into carbon-14 when it is hit by high energy particles, such as during a nuclear blast. Therefore an organism that died shortly before humanity started exploding nuclear warheads will appear to have died long after any organism that has died since we started exploding them. Naturally, while this may be confusing to our distant descendants, it does not impact Egyptology, however, there are other sources of high energy particles that occasionally cause spikes in the amount of carbon-14 in our atmosphere. One of these sources is cosmic rays, which are believed to be the main ongoing source of new carbon-14, however, for some reason the amount of cosmic rays occasionally spikes, causing spikes in the amount of carbon-14 in the atmosphere.

Scientists have been examining very old trees since the 1970s in an attempt to calibrate carbon-testing. Tree-rings have been used for centuries to work out the ancient environment of the planet, as trees grow better in warm and moist years, leaving thicker rings for those years. Because some species of trees can live for thousands of years, continuous tree-ring timelines have been worked out going back to 12,460 years ago.[18] By carbon-dating samples from these tree-rings, scientists have found points in the time when major volcanic eruptions have happened, and more recently when major spikes in carbon-14 have happened. In 2012 a cosmic-ray spike was found in tree-ring samples from 774-775 AD,[19] another was found in 2017 from 3372-3371 BC,[20] and another was also found in 2017 from 5480 BC.[21] Each time one of these cosmic-ray spikes is found it requires the calibration curve to be adjusted, and therefore all carbon-dates from before the cosmic-

---

[18] M. Friedrich, et al. (2004) "The 12,460-year Hohenheim oak and pine tree-ring chronology from central Europe - A unique annual record for radiocarbon calibration and paleoenvironment reconstructions," *Radiocarbon*, 46 (3): 1111-22

[19] Kimiaki Masuda (27 July 2012) "A signature of cosmic-ray increase in AD 774-775 from tree rings in Japan," *Nature*, Volume 486, Pages 240-

[20] F. Y. Wang, et al. (14 Nov 2017) "A rapid cosmic-ray increase in BC 3372-3371 from ancient buried tree rings in China," *Nature Communications*, 8: 1487

[21] Fusa Miyake (Jan 31, 2017) "Large 14C excursion in 5480 BC indicates an abnormal sun in the mid-Holocene," *Proceedings of the National Academy of Sciences*, 114 (5) 881-884

ray spike need to be updated. This constantly fluctuating dendro-timeline is the reason why most Egyptologists haven't embraced carbon-dating.

Additionally, as people have lived in Egypt throughout all of Egyptian history, and people have been obsessed with old artifacts throughout all of human history, older artifacts have been routinely dug up and then deposited with later debris. This means that when artifacts are found they cannot be definitively dated by the debris they are found with. It also means that it is easy for Egyptologists to dismiss any radiocarbon dating results that deviate from the CET. The views of Egyptologists regarding scientific methods, such as carbon dating were well stated by Felix Höflmayer of the Austrian Academy of Sciences, Institute for Oriental and European Archaeology in 2016:

> *"The historical timeline of Egypt is a political timeline, and as such it is a priori independent from archaeological phases and sites' stratigraphies, material culture such as pottery, or scientific dating approaches, that is, radiocarbon dating."[22]*

A political history, independent from science or facts? Ah yes: fiction, that explains the time-traveling Hyksos.

---

[22] Felix Höflmayer (July 2016) Radiocarbon Dating and Egyptian timeline - From the 'Curve of Knowns' to Bayesian Modeling, Page 2

Part 2 - Pre-Dynastic Egypt

Before the dynastic period, Manetho and other ancient sources stated there was a series of older civilizations in the Nile. Little has been found from the period, however, some findings do support his claims. While much of the Pre-Dynastic era may be fiction, it would be irresponsible to propose returning to Manetho's timeline without looking at what the Egyptians believed came before.

PRE-DYNASTIC EGYPTIAN TIMELINE		
Period	**Manetho**	**Turin**
Reign of the gods		53,155 to 29,955 BC
Kings from Horus to Bydis	30,435 to 16,535 BC	29,955 to 16,535 BC
Demigods	16,535 to 15,280 BC	
1817-year-long rule of kings	15,280 to 13,463 BC	
30 kings of Memphis	13,463 to 11,673 BC	
10 kings of Thinis	11,673 to 11,323 BC	
Spirits of the Dead and Demigods	11,323 to 5510 BC	

Zep Tepi

One might read the history of Christian scholars re-writing Egyptian history, and wonder why? What difference does it make when the Ancient Egyptians thought their civilization was founded to a Christian? If someone believes the world was created in 4004 BC, what difference does it make if ancient Egyptians thought their civilization was founded in 5510 BC? After all, they weren't Christian. The reason early Christians were so insistent on re-dating the ancient Egyptian timeline, was because it was tied directly to the Egyptian concept of Zep Tepi, or the First Time.

The First Time was what came before the unification of Egypt at the beginning of the 1st Dynasty. Zep Tepi was a time when Gods and Spirits ruled Egypt, and this brought it into direct conflict with early Christianity, and the idea that there was only one God. This obsession with 'proving Christianity' continued to be mainstream thought well into the 1900s, although it is now generally not a concern to academics, other than to the 'agnostic' David Rohl.

Nevertheless, modern Egyptologists continue to ignore Zep Tepi, as their Christian precursors did, using the same reasoning: those gods and spirits didn't exist, so why bother studying them? It seems strange that people who have dedicated their lives to studying ancient Egypt would simply not bother studying parts of Egyptian history based on their personal assumptions that these parts of history didn't happen, yet that is the state of current Egyptology. Whatever the ancient Egyptians were trying to remember and record in their history, is apparently not important to modern Egyptologists, which is why the CET can be not only the dominant time-line but only timeline studied by Egyptologists, when it directly contradicts the records of the ancient Egyptians.

This arrogance regarding recent assumptions is ubiquitous in modern history, where it is considered appropriate to dismiss all ancient records predating 3000 to 4000 BC. Most historians go so far as to claim these ancient records do not exist at all, yet, they clearly do. Whether they are accurate or non-sensical, the ancient Mesopotamians had records going back to over 200,000 years ago. The Avesta, the religious holy book of the Zoroastrian faith, includes a reference to the Arctic before the last glacial period began circa 130,000 years ago and a description of the onset of the glaciers that destroyed that world. The oldest sections of the Rig-Veda, a Hindu holy book, are believed to date to around the same age as the Avesta, as the two languages used are virtually identical. Other Hindu holy books contain histories that apparently go back millions of years. And in Egypt, there was Zep Tepi, the First Time.

The records of Zep Tepi are even more fragmentary than the records of the Old Kingdom, however, should be considered, when considering the roots of Egyptian history. That the ancient Egyptians believed that their civilization was originally founded by, and ruled by gods cannot be disputed, as these gods show up in ancient Egyptian king lists, such as the Turin King List from circa 1250 BC. The Turin King List is a list of kings that lived in ancient Egypt up until the New Kingdom when it was compiled. It was written on a piece of papyrus, which was miraculously preserved in the Egyptian desert for thousands of years, and then quickly deteriorated once taken to the humid climate of Italy. The part of the papyrus that was damaged the worst was the beginning of the king list which dealt with the Zep Tepi.

All that remains of that section is a few scattered fragments and the summation at the bottom of the section. This summation is generally restored as:

Reign of Spirits and Followers of Horus
13,420 years,

their lifetime until the Followers of Horus,
23,200 years.[23]

This reference to the Reign of Spirits and Followers of Horus seems to be a reference to what Manetho recorded in the Aegyptiaca regarding the Zep Tepi. In Aegyptiaca, Manetho recorded that before the unification of Egypt in 5510 BC, Egypt was ruled by a series of gods, followed by a series of human, spirit, and demigod rulers. The sequence as recorded as Eusebius follows along with his first draft of the short-timeline:

THE AEGYPTIACA OF MANETHO:
MANETHO'S HISTORY OF EGYPT

Excerpted from the Eusebius' Chronica

BOOK I.

Reign of Spirits and Followers of Horus

---

[23] Wolfgang Helck (1992) "Anmerkungen zum Turiner Königspapyrus," *Studien zur Altägyptischen Kultur* 19: 151–216.

Dynasties of Gods, Demigods, and Spirits of the Dead.

From the Egyptian History of Manetho, who composed his account in three books. These deal with the Gods, the Demigods, the Spirits of the Dead, and the mortal kings who ruled Egypt down to Darius, king of the Persians.

1. The first man [or god] in Egypt is Hephaestus [Ptah], who is also renowned among the Egyptians as the discoverer of fire. His son, Helios [Ra], was succeeded by Sosis [Shu]: then follow, in turn, Cronos [Geb], Osiris, Typhon [Set], brother of Osiris, and lastly Orus [Horus], son of Osiris and Isis, These were the first to hold sway in Egypt. Thereafter, the kingship passed from one to another in unbroken succession down to Bydis through 13,900 years. The year I take, however, to be a lunar one, consisting, that is, of 30 days : what we now call a month the Egyptians used formerly to style a year.

2. After the Gods, Demigods reigned for 1255 years, and again another line of kings held sway for 1817 years: then came thirty more kings of Memphis, reigning for 1790 years; and then again ten kings of This [Thinis], reigning for 350 years.

3. There followed the rule of Spirits of the Dead and Demigods, for 5813 years.

4. The total [of the last five groups] amounts to 11,000 years, these however being lunar periods, or months. But, in truth, the whole rule of which the Egyptians tell — the rule of Gods, Demigods, and Spirits of the Dead — is reckoned to have comprised in all 24,900 lunar years, which make 2206 solar years.

5. *Now, if you care to compare these figures with Hebrew timeline, you will find that they are in perfect harmony. Egypt is called Mestraim by the Hebrews; and Mestraim lived not long after the Flood. For after the Flood, Cham (or Ham), son of Noah, begat Aegyptus or Mestraim, who was the first to set out to establish himself in Egypt, at the time when the tribes began to disperse this way and that. Now the whole time from Adam to the Flood was, according to the Hebrews, 2242 years.*

6. *But, since the Egyptians claim by a sort of prerogative of antiquity that they have, before the Flood, a line of Gods, Demigods, and Spirits of the Dead, who reigned for more than 20,000 years, it clearly follows that these years should be reckoned as the same number of months as the years recorded by the Hebrews: that is, that all the months contained in the Hebrew record of years, should be reckoned as so many lunar years of the Egyptian calculation, in accordance with the total length of time reckoned from the creation of man in the beginning down to Mestraim. Mestraim was indeed the founder of the Egyptian race; and from him the first Egyptian dynasty must be held to spring.*

7. *But if the number of years is still in excess, it must be supposed that perhaps several Egyptian kings ruled at one and the same time; for they say that the rulers were kings of This, of Memphis, of Sals, of Ethiopia, and of other places at the same time. It seems, moreover, that different kings held sway in different regions, and that each dynasty was confined to its own nome : thus it was not a succession of kings occupying the throne one after the other, but several kings reigning at the same time in different regions. Hence arose the*

great total number of years. But let us leave this question and take up in detail the timeline of Egyptian history."

Modern Egyptologists entirely reject the idea that the Egyptians didn't know the difference between months and years, however, his multiple concurrent dynasties hypothesis managed to return to mainstream Egyptology after being thoroughly debunked in the 1800s. Regardless of Eusebius' intent, he did leave us one of the few large excerpts of Manetho. His interpretation of Manetho attempts to compress Manetho's timeline to 24,900 years, then further compresses it to 2206 years to make it fit into the 'Hebrew timeline,' that the Christians were trying to convert everyone to in the first few centuries of the Christian Era. However Manetho didn't state that the History of Egypt was 24,900 years long, he stated there were 24,925 years between the rule of Horus and the beginning of the 1st Dynasty, circa 5510 BC. This breaks down as:

1. Unspecified length of time when the gods ruled,

2. 13,900-year-long chain of kings from Horus to Bydis,

3. 1255-year-long rule of demigods,

4. 1817-year-long rule of kings,

5. 1790-year-long rule of 30 kings of Memphis,

6. 350-year-long rule of 10 kings of Thinis (This),

7. 5813-year-long rule of the Spirits of the

Dead and Demigods,

8. 5510 BC beginning of the 1st Dynasty.

The last of the gods to rule was Horus according to Manetho, followed by the 13,900-year-long rule of the kings ending with Bydis, which seems to be a near-parallel with the 13,420-year-long rule of the 'Spirits and Followers of Horus' recorded in the Turin King List. This would mean that the rule of the gods would be 23,200 years long, as recorded in the Turin King List, placing the beginning of the rule of Ptah the first god at approximately 53,155 to 53,635 BC. Manetho was clearly using a different source than the Turin papyrus, however, the difference of 480 years, or 3.5%, is quite insignificant considering the tremendous time-span being described.

According to Manetho the 13,900-year-long period of rule by kings ending with Bydis, was followed by the rule of demigods for 1255 years, then another line of kings for 1817 years, followed by thirty more kings based in Memphis who reigned for 1790 years, and then again ten kings based in Thinis, who reigned for 350 years. Thinis was then followed by the rule of spirits of the dead and demigods for 5813 years, followed by the unification of Egypt, in 5510 BC.

These additional 'dynasties' between the 'Spirits and Followers of Horus' and the Old Kingdom are missing from the Turin King List, however, given the condition of the papyrus, it is not surprising. Adding all these gods, demigods, and 'archaic dynasties' together pushes back the foundation of Egypt to 53,635 BC. This is a completely different concept than Egypt being founded either circa 5510 or 3100 BC. If there is any truth in this claim of extreme antiquity to Egypt, it changes not only our concept of Egyptian history but our understanding of civilization itself.

How would anyone prove that Egypt is older than... Egypt? One could look into the archaeological record for any evidence of older structures, however, all known ancient structures in Egypt have already been attributed to the dynastic period even when there are no records of them being built. While there are those who believe the sphinx, megalithic temples, and even the great pyramids date back to predynastic times, using them as evidence is problematic, as they are already generally accepted as being dynastic in origin. Perhaps it would be best to start with the dates recorded by Manetho and see if anything was happening in Egypt at the time.

Rule of Spirits of the Dead and Demigods

The era that directly preceded the 1st Dynasty in Aegyptiaca was the so-called 'rule of spirits of the dead and demigods' which lasted for 5813 years. 5813 years before 5510 BC was approximately 13,323 years ago. Archaeological evidence has been found of several cultures in the Nile during the time period, the Isnan, Sebilian, and Qadan cultures, all of which lived in southern Egypt at the time. The Isnan and Sebilian cultures were essentially destroyed by the so-called 'Wild-Nile' period, while the Qadan was severely damaged, and ultimately faded away a few centuries later.

The Wild-Nile was a period late in the Late Paleolithic when the glaciers of the Ethiopian highlands were melting, which resulted in significantly higher annual floods than later periods in Egyptian history. This was particularly bad circa 13,500 years ago, when there were also heavy rains in Central Africa, which caused Lake Victoria to overflow, sending massive amounts of water up the White Nile. These annual floods were averaging between 5 and 10 meters higher than during dynastic times and deposited a great deal of sediment along the shores of the Nile. Many Sebilian settlements are buried in over 25 meters of flood deposits. This period of extreme and erratic annual floods began around 13,500 years ago, and continued, decreasing in magnitude, until shortly before the beginning of the dynastic era.

The time has been described as the most important catastrophic event in the Late Pleistocene history of the Nile,[24] and caused the Nile to be virtually abandoned for thousands of years until shortly before the beginning of the 1st Dynasty. This actually does sound like something that could be described poetically as the 'rule of spirits of the dead and demigods,' if one accepts that the Egyptians of the time didn't know why the Nile god was behaving so chaotically and blamed it on demigods.

---

[24] Pierre M.Vermeerscha and WimVan Neer (2015) *Quaternary Science Reviews*, Volume 130, Pages 155-167

The 10 Kings of Thinis

Prior to the 'rule of the spirits of the dead,' was the rule of 'ten kings of This,' who reigned for 350 years. The city of This, also called Tjenu or Thinis, is a pre-dynastic city that is believed to exist in the region of Abydos by Egyptologists, however, has never been found. It is almost certainly the 7300-year-old village found in the vicinity of Abydos in 2016, but Egyptologists need it to date to around 5100 years ago for their timeline to work, so they'll have to keep looking for it.

It is mentioned in many early texts, and according to Manetho was the home-town of King Menes who founded the 1st Dynasty in 5510 BC. It is believed to have been in the vicinity of ancient Abydos, modern Girga. If the records of there being a dynasty based in Thinis between 13,673 and 13,323 years ago are correct, then there should be some archaeological evidence, and there is.

While it cannot be definitively proven yet that the Qadan Culture had anything to do with the city later called Thinis, it was in the general vicinity of where Thinis is believed to have later been. Without having officially discovered the ruins of Thinis, it is impossible to conduct excavations which could determine its age, therefore we cannot know if Thinis was rebuilt on the ruins of an older city, however, it is clear that there was a culture between 14,000 and 13,500 years ago in the vicinity of where Thinis would eventually stand, the Qadan culture. It is difficult to imagine how Manetho could have known this, nevertheless, the archaeology does support at least the possibility that there was an archaic dynasty in the region of

Thinis, between 14,000 and 13,500 years ago.

Naturally given its age, and the massive flooding that followed its demise, very little remains from the Qadan culture. The Qadan culture seems to have been a hunter-gatherer society that largely survived on the wild grains that grew in the Nile valley, and hunted and fished along the shores of the Nile. Based on remains exhumed from cemeteries, the Qadan people used projectile weapons, including spears, slings, and bows and arrows.[25] This culture seems to have been very warlike, as most of the exhumed remains show signs of damage inflicted by weapons. It is unclear who they were fighting.

The culture itself is believed to have started around 15,000 years ago in northern Sudan, and then slowly spread north up the Nile. The region around Thinis was likely as far north as the culture spread and would have only been present in the region for a few centuries before the Wild-Nile period started, which would have effectively ended the settlement near Abydos. Once the Wild-Nile period began the battered Qadan culture shrank back to its cultural hearth in southernmost Egypt, where it slowly weathered until disappearing sometime around 12,000 years ago.

---

[25] Facts On File, Incorporated (2009) *Encyclopedia of the Peoples of Africa and the Middle East.* Page 777

The 30 Kings of Memphis

According to Manetho, before the rule of the 10 Kings of Thinis, there was a dynasty of 30 kings based in Memphis who ruled for 1790 years. The location of the dynastic city of Memphis is known, it's near the modern town of Mit Rahina, 20 km south of Giza. The city of Memphis was the capital of the Egyptian Old Kingdom, said to have been founded by King Menes after he unified Egypt circa 5510 BC ULT (or 3100 BC CET). It was a major city throughout most of Egyptian history and is the root of where the name 'Egypt' is derived. While the city of Memphis founded by Menes could be at the location of the earlier city of Memphis, it is not necessarily the case.

The name Memphis is derived from the ancient Egyptian words 'Hut-ka-Ptah,' meaning 'Enclosure of the ka of Ptah.' The term 'ka of Ptah' translates as essentially the 'spirit of Ptah,' or more literally 'craftsmen,' as Ptah was the patron deity of craftsmen. Therefore the name of the city could be read as the 'enclosure,' or 'fortress' of the craftsmen. This basic term is found in several ancient cultures across the region, such as the ancient Sumerian Bad-tibira, which also meant 'fortress' of the smiths or craftsmen. Like the Egyptian city of Memphis, Bad-tibira was both a historic city in Iraq and an ancient quasi-mythical city from a time period thousands of years before the foundation of Sumer. This concept of the 'city of the smiths,' whatever it might have originally meant, is so ingrained in the ancient Middle Eastern culture that it even found its way into the Tanakh (Biblical Old Testament). In the earliest part of the Bible, the first city was built by Cain, the first metalsmith.

Naturally, it is possible that King Menes built his capital where he thought the ancient city of Memphis was, however, there is no reason to assume that he did. If one does assume that Menes' Memphis was in the vicinity of the ancient Memphis, then one faces the fact that Menes' Memphis was in the area that is today covered by modern Greater Cairo. Finding the original Memphis under all that might not be possible.

According to Manetho, this dynasty should have existed between 15,463 and 13,673 years ago, presumably in the Greater Cairo area. While there were several different cultures known to have been in southern Egypt during the period in question, in northern Egypt, there is virtually nothing known. The reason for this is that the average depth of the Nile is significantly higher today than it was 15,000 years ago. Currently, the average depth of the Nile north of Cairo is less than 1 meter higher than the Mediterranean Sea, however, 15,000 years ago the Mediterranean was over 100 meters lower than it is today. Between 14,700 and 13,500 years ago the global ocean level is believed to have increased around 25 meters due to the melting of glaciers. Therefore if there was any culture along the Nile in northern Egypt between 15,463 and 13,673 years ago, it would have been drowned as the ocean levels rose and caused the Nile depth to rise. Unless this very early Memphite dynasty built something inland, away from the Nile, whatever they built could now be 70 to 100 meters below the ground-level of Cairo.

For thousands of years, there have been rumors of an underground city in the region of Memphis that dates back to 15,000 years ago, however, there have been no recent archaeological digs that support this. One site does look promising, the rumored underground labyrinth reported by the ancient Greek historian Herodotus circa 450 BC in the Fayum depression, near Lake Moeris. Herodotus recorded the labyrinth in *The Histories, Book 2: Euterpe*, 148-149:

> *"148. Moreover they resolved to join all together and leave a memorial of themselves; and having so resolved they caused to be made a labyrinth, situated a little above the lake of Moiris and nearly opposite to that which is called the City of Crocodiles. This I saw myself, and I found it greater than words can say. For if one should put together and reckon up all the buildings and all the great works produced by the Hellenes, they would prove to be inferior in labour and expense to this labyrinth, though it is true that both the temple at Ephesos and that at Samos are works worthy of note. The pyramids also were greater than words can say, and each one of them is equal to many works of the Hellenes, great as they may be; but the labyrinth surpasses even the pyramids. It has twelve courts covered in, with gates facing one another, six upon the North side and six upon the South, joining on one to another, and the same wall surrounds them all outside; and there are in it two kinds of chambers, the one kind below the ground and the other above upon these, three thousand in number, of each kind fifteen hundred. The upper set of chambers we ourselves saw, going through them, and we tell of them having looked upon them with our own eyes; but the chambers under ground we*

heard about only; for the Egyptians who had charge of them were not willing on any account to show them, saying that here were the sepulchres of the kings who had first built this labyrinth and of the sacred crocodiles. Accordingly we speak of the chambers below by what we received from hearsay, while those above we saw ourselves and found them to be works of more than human greatness. For the passages through the chambers, and the goings this way and that way through the courts, which were admirably adorned, afforded endless matter for marvel, as we went through from a court to the chambers beyond it, and from the chambers to colonnades, and from the colonnades to other rooms, and then from the chambers again to other courts. Over the whole of these is a roof made of stone like the walls; and the walls are covered with figures carved upon them, each court being surrounded with pillars of white stone fitted together most perfectly; and at the end of the labyrinth, by the corner of it, there is a pyramid of forty fathoms, upon which large figures are carved, and to this there is a way made under ground.

149. Such is this labyrinth; but a cause for marvel even greater than this is afforded by the lake, which is called the lake of Moiris, along the side of which this labyrinth is built. The measure of its circuit is three thousand six hundred furlongs (being sixty schoines), and this is the same number of furlongs as the extent of Egypt itself along the sea. The lake lies extended lengthwise from North to South, and in depth where it is deepest it is fifty fathoms. That this lake is artificial and formed by digging is self-evident, for about in the middle of the lake stand two pyramids, each

rising above the water to a height of fifty fathoms, the part which is built below the water being of just the same height; and upon each is placed a colossal statue of stone sitting upon a chair. Thus the pyramids are a hundred fathoms high; and these hundred fathoms are equal to a furlong of six hundred feet, the fathom being measured as six feet or four cubits, the feet being four palms each, and the cubits six. The water in the lake does not come from the place where it is, for the country there is very deficient in water, but it has been brought thither from the Nile by a canal: and for six months the water flows into the lake, and for six months out into the Nile again; and whenever it flows out, then for the six months it brings into the royal treasury a talent of silver a day from the fish which are caught, and twenty pounds when the water comes in."

Herodotus' description of the Fayum depression being artificial is partially correct because although it is a natural depression, it was artificially terraced by the Middle Kingdom, creating what almost all ancient authors described to be an artificial lake region. The Roman-era historian Strabo was one of the few classical historians who claimed it was a natural formation. The Labyrinth he described was dismantled in the Greco-Roman era, so the stone could be used to build new buildings in Alexandria and Memphis. The site of the labyrinth was discovered by W. M. Flinders Petrie in 1889, who described it in *Ten Years Digging in Egypt*, pages 91-92:

"Though the pyramid was the main object at Hawara, it was but a lesser part of my work there. On the south of the pyramid lay a wide mass of chips and fragments of building, which

had long generally been identified with the celebrated labyrinth. Doubts, however, existed, mainly owing to Lepsius having considered the brick buildings on the site to have been part of the labyrinth.

When I began to excavate the result was soon plain, that the brick chambers were built on the top of the ruins of a great stone structure; and hence they were only the houses of a village, as they had at first appeared to me to be. But beneath them, and far away over a vast area, the layers of stone chips were found; and so great was the mass that it was difficult to persuade visitors that the stratum was artificial, and not a natural formation. Beneath all these fragments was a uniform smooth bed of beton or plaster, on which the pavement of the building had been laid: while on the south side, where the canal had cut across the site, it could be seen how the chip stratum, about six feet thick, suddenly ceased, at what had been the limits of the building.

No trace of architectural arrangement could be found, to help in identifying this great structure with the labyrinth: but the mere extent of it proved that it was far larger than any temple known in Egypt. All the temples of Karnak, of Luxor, and a few on the western side of Thebes, might be placed together within the vast space of these buildings at Hawara. We know from Pliny and others, how for centuries the labyrinth had been a great quarry for the whole district; and its destruction occupied such a body of masons, that a small town existed there. All this information, and the recorded position of it, agrees so closely with what we can trace, that no doubt can now remain regarding the position of one of the *wonders of Egypt."*

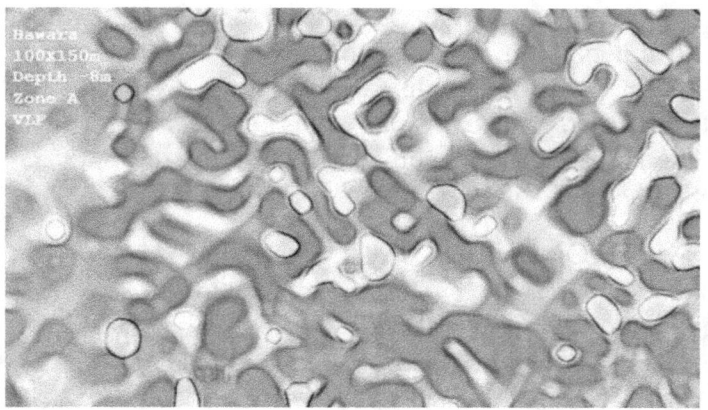

In 2008 a group of Belgian and Egyptian researchers using ground-penetrating radar discovered that this massive stone platform that Petrie's team discovered does, in fact, have a lower level that appears to contain hundreds of large regularly spaced rooms, approximately 8 to 12 meters below the surface. So far they have not found the entrance to the lower level, which was fortunately well hidden. The team published their results in Egypt's *National Research Institute of Astronomy and Geophysics* (NRIAG), however, shortly afterward the Secretary-General of the Supreme Council of Antiquities in Egypt put a stop to all communications regarding the labyrinth, apparently due to Egyptian National Security sanctions.

The strange underground labyrinth exists on both sides of the modern Bahr Wahbi canal, encompassing the entire Hawara region south of the Hawara pyramid, which Herodotus referred to as one of the labyrinth's corners. Unfortunately, the water level has increased significantly since the labyrinth must have been built, as today the mean water level in the Fayum is only 4 meters below ground level in the Hawara region, meaning the entire subterranean labyrinth must be submerged, as it lays 8 to 12 meters below ground level.

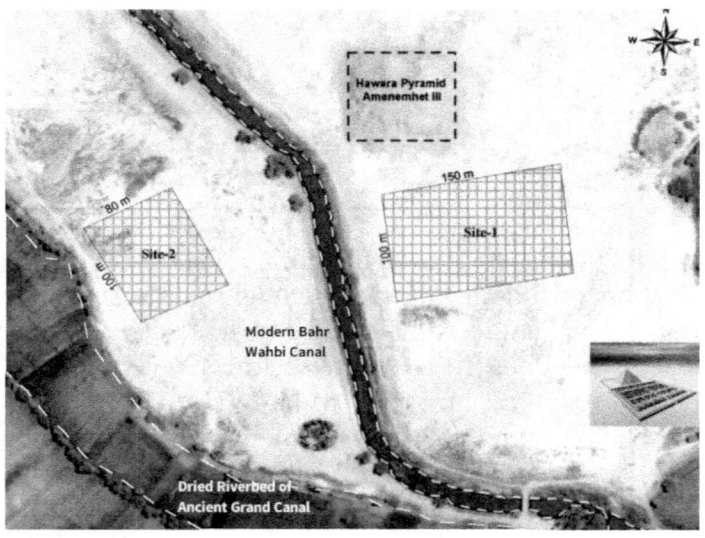

The average water level in the Fayum is significant when considering when this labyrinth was built, as it has to predate the modern high level of water in the Fayum, and naturally had to predate the time of Herodotus. Nevertheless, in the time of Herodotus, the water level was even higher than today, statues that he claimed were out in the lake were discovered in the 1800s miles from the shore of the lake, which had shrunk significantly during the intervening 2300 years. This means the priests at the labyrinth that refused to give Herodotus access to the lower level, couldn't have given him access even if they'd wanted to, as the area would have been filled with water even back then.

This means that we need to look back in time to see when the Fayum had significantly less water than it does now, in order to determine when the underground labyrinth was built. The area was extensively altered during the Middle Kingdom when the Pyramid of Hawara was built. The terraces surrounding the lake were built, and the canal linking the Fayum to the Nile was dug, allowing the Nile floods to fill Lake Qarun in Fayum each year. This massive project to rebuild the Fayum to the productivity level of the Old Kingdom era seems to have been the primary focus of the Middle Kingdom. The Pyramid of Hawara is recorded as being built by Amenemhat III, during the 12th Dynasty, who is also recorded to have dug the Grand Canal connecting the Fayum to the Nile.

Clearly, the subterranean labyrinth could not have been built after the Fayum was flooded, and therefore it had to have been built sometime before Amenemhat III's reign. Creating the Grand Canal was, in fact, more of a dredging operation, clearing debris from the Bahr Yussef channel that had connected the Nile and Fayum during the African Humid period, prior to 6000 years ago. During this earlier period, the Fayum was flooded annually by the Nile floods, and the lake in the Fayum was significantly deeper than either today or during Herodotus' time.

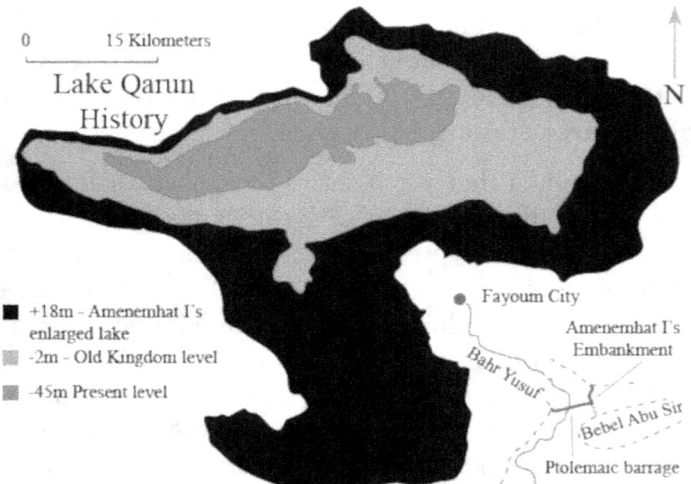

0   15 Kilometers

Lake Qarun
History

N

■ +18m - Amenemhat I's
enlarged lake
▦ -2m - Old Kingdom level
▦ -45m Present level

● Fayoum City

Amenemhat I's
Embankment

Bahr Yussuf

Bebel Abu Sir

Ptolemaic barrage

This means that the subterranean labyrinth was either built after the water levels dropped, sometime between 6000 years ago and the 12th Dynasty, or significantly earlier. Therefore knowing when the Old and Middle Kingdoms were, is extremely important when considering this ancient labyrinth's construction. Theoretically, if the Old Kingdom existed between 2686 and 2181 BC as the CET states, then the Bahr Yussef channel should have been dried out, and the water level in the Fayum should have been very low, leaving a dried out region. However, this is not what Old Kingdom sources record. The Fayum region was known to during the Old Kingdom as Ta-She meaning the 'Land of the Lakes.' It was a lush land where the Kings from Memphis went hunting. It was in fact far more humid than during the later Middle Kingdom, indicating that either the Bahr Yussef was open, or there was rain in the region or both. In fact, Egyptologists believe that the water level in the Fayum was over 40 meters higher in the

104

Old Kingdom than it is today. This is further evidence for the ULT being correct.

Nevertheless, whether the Old Kingdom was between 2686 and 2181 BC CET or 4945 and 4003 BC ULT, the Fayum was flooded and fertile, meaning that the water level was high. The labyrinth could not have been built during the First Intermediate Period, as it is described as being larger than all the Old Kingdom and Middle Kingdom temples combined. This means that it was either built during the first few centuries of the Middle Kingdom, or much, much earlier. The first 150 years of the Middle Kingdom was focused on the war of reunification, and it seems unlikely that they would have built a massive labyrinth near the border between the competing kingdoms, therefore it was either built during the first century of the 12th Dynasty or much, much earlier.

Between the reunification of Egypt at the beginning of the 12th Dynasty circa 3459 BC ULT (1991 BC CET), and Amenemhat III becoming King in 3328 BC ULT (1860 BC CET) were the reigns of five kings. Each of these kings engaged in major pyramid building works, however, only one is associated with the Fayum before Amenemhat III. Amenemhet III's grandfather Senusret II built the Pyramid at El-Lahun in the Fayum, however, unlike most other pyramids at the time, this one wasn't built with bricks, but with packed mud. Clearly, the Fayum wasn't dried out before the reopening of the Bahr Yussef channel, as no one would carry mud into the desert to build a pyramid, when there were rocks nearby that could be quarried. The mud must have been locally sourced, which means the Fayum wasn't dry, and Amenemhet III's projects in the Fayum and Bahr Yussef were intended to increase the local food production, not create a lake land from a desert.

This means that there is no point in dynastic Egyptian history when the subterranean labyrinth could have been constructed, meaning we have to look back to a much earlier point. Regardless of when the Old and Middle Kingdoms were, the Fayum was too wet for the subterranean labyrinth to have been built then, therefore, we have look to the paleoclimatological record to see when the water level in the Fayum was low enough for the labyrinth to have been built. We know it could not have been during the African Humid Period which spanned ap-proximately 14,600 to 6,000 years ago, as there was both high water flow down the Nile that would have flooded the Fayum each year, and heavy rainfall, which would have also flooded the Fayum. This means that the labyrinth could have only been built before the onset of the African Humid Period, before 14,600 years ago, which is consistent with Manetho's 30 Kings of Memphis. The paleoclimatological record also shows that prior to the onset of the African Hu-mid Period, Egypt was very dry, and the water level would have been significantly lower than in later pe-riods.

Clearly, any civilization capable of building a labyrinth that was larger than all the temples and palaces of the Greek kingdoms combined had to be a significant civilization. Perhaps if Egyptologists ever acquire the technology to examine the region of Cairo 70-100 meters below the current ground level, an ancient city of Memphis from circa 15,000 years ago will be found, however, it is equally possible that the labyrinth in the Fayum is the ancient city of Memphis.

The limited information gathered of the Labyrinth from ground-penetrating radar does not look like the majority of Egyptian architecture, however, it does resemble a couple of strange structures. The apparent use of large solid blocks of stone weighing tonnes as square columns does match the architecture in the Osireion and the red quartzite Valley Temple of Giza. The Osireion is a strange subterranean temple next to the Temple of Seti I, in Abydos. The upper level of the Osireion was excavated in 1925, and is no longer subterranean, however, it was when Strabo visited it sometime before he described it in *Geographica*, first published in 7 BC:

> *"Above this city [Ptolemaïs] lies Abydus, where is the Memnonium, a royal building, which is a remarkable structure built of solid stone, and of the same workmanship as that which I ascribed to the Labyrinth, though not multiplex; and also a fountain which lies at a great depth, so that one descends to it down vaulted galleries made of monoliths of surprising size and workmanship."*[26]

The Memnonium Strabo mentioned is the Temple of Seti I, his other name was Menmaatre, which was then used to reference his temple. The fountain Strabo mentions is the Osireion which he went on to claim was built by Amenemhet III since it was so much like the Labyrinth in the Fayum. Modern

---

[26] Strabo (7 BC) *Geographica*, 17.1.42

Egyptologists generally assume it was built at the same time as the Temple of Seti I from the New Kingdom, who ruled circa 1294 to 1279 BC. The Osireion is today partially below the water table, as it was during the life of Strabo 2000 years ago, and as it was during the life of Seti I 3250 years ago. Historically the water table was higher during Strabo's time than it is today and even higher during the time of Seti I. How exactly the ancient Egyptians built a subterranean structure underwater, and why it was built in a very different style than almost every other structure in Egypt, is generally ignored by Egyptologists.

The previous image demonstrates the massive solid quartzite stones used in the construction of the Osireion. The obvious differences between the construction techniques of the Osireion and the Temple of Seti I have been noted since early Egyptologists began studying the Osireion. In 1914 Swiss Egyptologist Henri Édouard Naville published a paper in The Journal of Egyptian Archaeology, in which he described the uncovering of the Osireion, and gave his opinion on the structure:

> *"When we reached the end of the passage, on both sides we found wide openings which evidently were chambers, and in front a huge monolithic lintel 15 feet long. It looked at first like an entrance to another passage, but we soon perceived that it was merely an opening in a stone wall about 12 feet thick, built of enormous blocks of sandstone and red quartzite. This wall separates the two rooms we had first reached from other rooms in the direction of the temple. We could clear only the southern room. The west wall leans against a mound of marl and is thinner. The southern one has outside a kind of rough casing in limestone and I believe it was not subterranean at that place. The erection was roofed over with large stones which have been used since as building material. Over the roof was probably sand, so that the whole construction looked like a huge mastaba.*
>
> *The wall on the east side of the chamber is built of enormous stones very well joined. It reminds one of the masonry of the time of the pyramids, of the so-called Temple of the Sphinx. It seems probable that it is much older than the temple of Seti. It may have been part of the first sanctuary, for there was certainly one at an early date, at least of the time of the 12th dynasty. Otherwise one would not understand why there was such a large cemetery of that epoch, and of the following dynasty, such as is found in the hill called Kom-es-sultân, where Mariette made such productive excavations.*

Beyond this wall, going towards the temple, we could trace two more rooms, so that what we are now excavating is not a mere passage, it is a series of rooms, the last of which is probably under the temple of Seti.

This is one of the questions raised by this unique construction. Are we here in the oldest sanctuary of Osiris? For we cannot suppose that there was none at the time when the kings of the first dynasties built their funereal monuments at Umm el Ga'ab. There must have been a settlement of some importance in a place which already, at that early time, had a sacred character. This character would naturally be derived from the existence of a sanctuary, from its being the abode of a most venerated divinity.

Abydos has always been the city of Osiris, as Heliopolis was the city of Tum. When did Abydos begin to be the residence of the god? When was the first place of worship erected there, and when did Osiris take that name instead of Apuatu? I am going to risk an opinion which, I confess, is at present only a conjecture. The name of Osiris means "he who makes a seat or an abode," and Apuatu, as we have seen, is "the opener of ways," the guide whom the conquerors follow. Did the change of name not take place when an abode, a sanctuary, was first built at Abydos, and he ceased to be the wandering god, the standard of a tribe of migrating conquerors? If this hypothesis were confirmed, it would explain also why Abydos was the first capital of the early kings, and the starting point of Menes."[27]

---

[27] Edouard Naville (1914) "Excavations at Abydos: The Great Pool and the Tomb of Osiris," *The Journal of Egyptian Archaeology*, Volume 1

Prior to the upper level of the Osireion being excavated, it was filled with debris, as the roof stones had been quarried since the time of Strabo, and sand and rocks had filled the interior. Based on ancient descriptions it seems to have still been fully covered in the Greco-Roman era. This naturally brings up the question of what it was covered with. Naville postulated that it was originally built above ground level, and covered in sand, making it look like a giant mastaba. Mastabas were large flat-topped tombs built during the Old Kingdom that are believed to have evolved into pyramids during the 4th Dynasty, meaning Naville was proposing the Osireion dated to the earliest era in Egyptian dynastic history.

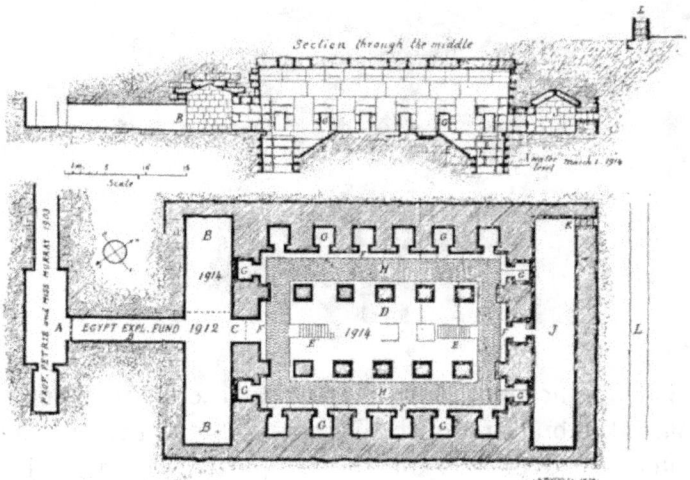

The Osireion was clearly known of when the Temple of Seti I was built, as they built around it and possibly on top of it, however, it was a known holy site for thousands of years before the time of Seti I.

The 13th Dynasty King Neferhotep I, circa 3237 BC ULT (1786 BC CET) during the Middle Kingdom era, erected a boundary stele at Abydos which it stated that none should set foot there. The region around the Osireion was also used extensively as a burial ground in the Old Kingdom, and back into pre-dynastic times. Clearly, the site was holy before Seti I built his New Kingdom Temple circa 1280 BC.

If one accepts the premise that the Osireion predates the building of the Temple of Seti I, then it was likely uncovered while the temple was being built. The land where the temple was built is an ancient floodplain, that was flattened out by digging out a level area for the temple to sit on. The floodplain was deposited by the Nile during the Wild-Nile period, meaning that the Osireion would need to date back to before 13,500 years ago when the massive Nile floods began. The previous photograph shows the Osireion and the floodplain layers behind it, which clearly would have covered the building if it was there before the flooding started.

Currently, only the upper level of the Osireion is excavated, as the lower levels are below the water level. Based on historical accounts and historic water levels of the nearby Nile, it is clear that this was the only level known to ancient visitors to the Osireion. Due to the water level, no attempts have been made to excavate down into lower levels, and the Osireion was assumed to be just what we now know is only the top level. The currently excavated top level is 13 meters below the surrounding ground level, and the channel in the middle of the Osireion was initially cleared another 4.3 meters in 1925, however, this was not the bottom of the Osireion, simply the level that could be cleared to with 1920's technology. In 2008 a paper was published that reported the soil in the channel had been successfully penetrated to 10.4 meters using a metal rod, and seismic data indicated that the wall of the channel may extend to 15 meters below the current water level.[28]

As the current water level fluctuates around 13 meters below ground level, and the Osireion's marble walls descent an estimated 15 meters below that, it means the Osireion's base must be at least 28 meters (90 feet) below the current ground level. While this area has not been excavated, Sebilian settle-

---

[28] J. S. Westerman (Jan 2008) "An Archaeological Analysis of the Osireion." *Third International Conference on the Geology of the Tethys, Aswan, Egypt*

ments south of Abydos have been excavated from under 25 meters of sediment dating the Wild-Nile phase, so the Osireion could have been buried around the same time, between 13,000 and 7500 years ago. If this structure was still above the surface of the then ground-level during the 10 Kings of Thinis era, between 11,673 and 11,323 BC, it could be why there was a dynasty based out of the Abydos region. In fact, there could be numerous structures buried in the region that just aren't tall enough for us to have stumbled across, from both the 10 Kings of Thinis, and earlier periods.

The fact that Naville stated the masonry looks older than the Temple of Seti I, and that is looked like the 'so-called Temple of the Sphinx' brings us back to the megalithic temples of the Giza Plateau. These two temples are today called the Sphinx Temple and the Valley Temple of Khafre. The Sphinx Temple is built directly in front of the Sphinx, east of the Sphinx between the Sphinx and the old Nile harbor. The Causeway of Khafre runs from the Pyramid of Khafre to the Sphinx Temple complex, where the harbor for the Khafre Causeway was located.

Naville's statement that the masonry of the Osireion looks like the 'so-called Temple of the Sphinx,' refers to the lower level of the Khafre's Valley Temple, which had not been distinguished from the adjacent Sphinx Temple during Naville's day. The two temples are immediately next to each other, however very little of the Sphinx Temple survives to the present, while a significant amount of the Khafre Valley Temple survives. The valley temple was built using two very different types of stone, and two very different construction techniques. The lower level was built using red quartzite, while the upper level was built using limestone, quarried on the Giza Plateau. The Sphinx Temple was built using limestone cut from the Sphinx enclosure. In both temples the surviving limestone blocks are heavily eroded after so many centuries, however, the quartzite blocks are still in remarkably good condition.

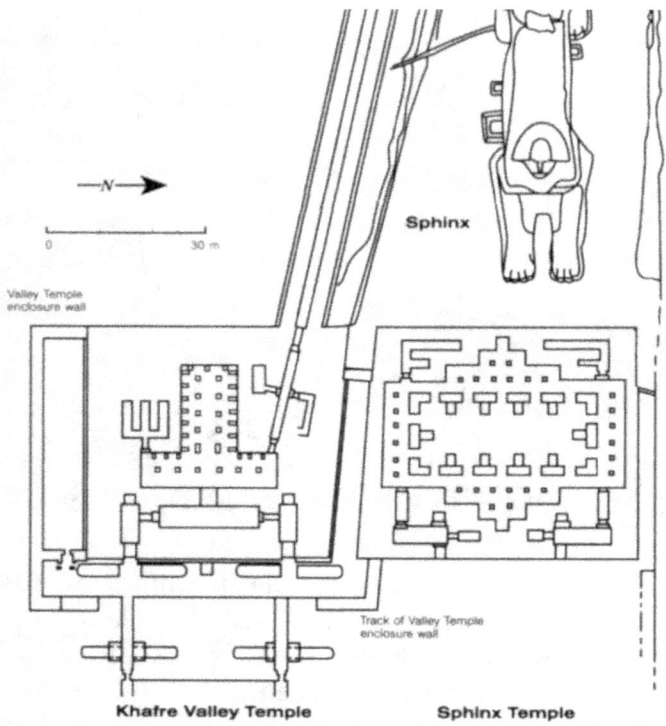

Khafre Valley Temple   **Sphinx Temple**

The reason for the lower level of the Khafre Valley Temple being built of a different stone is unknown, however, the remnants of the limestone Sphinx Temple directly to the north show a great deal of similarity of design, indicating whichever temple was built later seems to have been an expansion of the earlier temple. The style of the upper level of the valley temple does seem to be the same as the Khafre Mortuary Temple at the foot of the

Pyramid of Khafre, strongly indicating that the two temples and the causeway connecting them were built at the same time, presumably by Khafre. The name of Khafre was found in the debris at both the valley temple and mortuary temple,[29] and the pyramid's ancient Egyptian name was Wer(en)-Khafre, which translates as 'Khafre is Great,' which is why Egyptologists have decided that Khafre built the complex.

The Khafre Pyramid, Valley Temple, and Mortuary Temple, like the Khufu and Temple complexes, were built from limestone excavated from the Giza Plateau, pink-red granite from the Aswan quarries, and white limestone from the Tura quarries. The red quartzite of the lower level of the valley temple likely originated at the Red Mountain mines, where quartz, red quartzine, and red sandstone were mined in ancient times. The architecture is dramatically different from the rest of Giza, which has caused some Egyptologists to doubt if it is from the same period, or an earlier phase of construction that was adopted by Khafre. The view of early Egyptologists of the Khafre Valley Temple was summed up by Auguste Mariette in 1890:

> *"About six hundred yards to the S.E. of the Great Pyramid is the Sphinx. The Sphinx is a natural rock, to which has been given, more or less accurately, the external appearance of that mystic animal. The head alone has been sculptured. The body is formed of the rock itself,*

---

[29] Bertha Porter and Rosalind Moss (1974) *Topographical Bibliography of Ancient Egyptian Hieroglyphic Texts, Statues, Reliefs and Paintings Volume III: Memphis, Part I Abu Rawash to Abusir.* 2nd edition

supplemented, where defective, by a somewhat clumsy masonry of limestone. The total height of the monument is 19 metres, 80 centimetres, equal to 65 English feet. The ear measures 6 feet 5 inches; the nose 5 feet 10 inches; and the mouth 7 feet 8 inches. The face, in its widest part, across the cheek, is 4 metres 15 centimetres, that is 13 feet 7 inches. Its origin is still a matter of doubt. At one time it was supposed to be a monument of the reign of Thothmes IV (XVIIIth dynasty). But we know now, thanks to a stone in the 'Boolak Museum, that the Sphinx was already in existence when Cheops [Khufu] (who preceded Chephren [Khafre]) gave orders for the repairs which this stone commemorates. It must also be remembered that the Sphinx is the colossal image of an Egyptian god called Harmaehis.

Near the Sphinx is a singular construction which, even to a greater degree than the Sphinx itself, is an enigma to Egyptologists. It is certain that this construction is as ancient as the Pyramids. But is it a temple, or is it a tomb? Its external appearance, it must be confessed, is rather that of a tomb. From a distance it must have presented the appearance of a mastabah, scarcely exceeding in size those which are actually found, for example, at Abousir and Sakkdrah. In one of the chambers of the interior there are six compartments, place done above the other, which certainly seem to have been constructed, like those of the third Pyramid and of the Mastabat-el-Faraoun, for the reception of mummies. Moreover, the place does not differ essentially from that of certain other tombs which are found in the vicinity. It may therefore be fairly argued that the monument in question was a tomb, without violating any rules of *criticism; can the contrary opinion, which calls it a temple, be equally well supported? It is true, the Ancient Empire having left us no other temple with which to compare this one, it is not unnatural to suppose that at this remote period Egyptian temples might have been constructed on the extraordinary plan of the one we are now considering. Nor is it unnatural either to assume that, since the Sphinx is a god, the adjoining monument may be the temple of that god. But are these arguments sufficient? And, after all, to put the case plainly, is the monument an annex of the Sphinx, or is not rather the Sphinx an annex of the monument? Does not the whole of this represent a very ancient tomb, adorned, for the sake of greater dignity, with a colossal statue of a god? The question is pending."*

By the 1930s Egyptologists had generally agreed that the complex must have been built by Khafre, and so the pyramid, mortuary temple, causeway, and valley temple were all grouped together as 4th Dynasty buildings. The valley temple was connected to the mortuary temple at the foot of the pyramid via the causeway, and all of the buildings were built of locally sourced limestone, pink-red granite from the Aswan quarries, red quartzite from the Red Mountain quarries, and/or white limestone from the Tura quarries. The fact that the lower level of the valley temple was designed as a tomb and built in a different style of masonry was simply written off as an odd thing that once happened in Egypt. However, the question of the Sphinx Temple remained.

Only the lower level of the Sphinx Temple remains, and while the design is similar to the lower level of the valley temple, it is not made from red quartzite, but limestone quarried from the Sphinx enclosure. The Sphinx Temple shows no signs that it ever had stones quarried from Aswan, or Tura, or even the Giza Plateau other than the Sphinx enclosure. Comparative analysis of the surviving stones of the temple has even determined approximately where they were quarried from in the enclosure. This means that the Sphinx and Sphinx Temple, were made at the same time, and could have been produced by a local Giza culture, potentially long before the 4th Dynasty.

When Mariette asked the question of whether the Sphinx was an annex of the Khafre Valley Temple, or the Khafre Valley Temple was an annex of the Sphinx, it was because they appear to have been built at different points. The earliest Egyptologists to uncover the Sphinx believed it was built by the New Kingdom King Thutmose IV, circa 1400 BC who erected the Dream Stele between the paws of the Sphinx. This idea was overturned when the Inventory Stele was found in 1857 which stated that King Khufu of the 4th Dynasty had found the Sphinx buried in sand and restored it. The specific language of the Dream Stele was later determined to be Late-Egyptian and not Old-Egyptian and therefore the story can only be dated back to the New Kingdom or later, and is generally dated to the 26th Dynasty. It is possible that the story is a Late-Egyptian translation of an older story that may have originally been written in Old or Middle-Egyptian, and if nothing else proves that the ancient Egyptians of the Late Period believed the Sphinx predated the pyramids of Khufu and Khafre. Unfortunately, without any documentation of who built the Sphinx prior to Thutmose IV's claims of uncovering it during the New Kingdom, Egyptologists have been left with no recourse but to including it in with the Khafre structures, which clearly are designed to fit together. The situation was described by Hassan in 1949:

> *"Taking all things into consideration, it seems that we must give the credit of erecting this, the world's most wonderful statue, to Khafre, but always with this reservation: that there is not one single contemporary inscription which connects the Sphinx with Khafre; so, sound as it may appear, we must treat the evidence as circumstantial, until such time as a lucky turn of the spade of the excavator will reveal to the world a definite reference to the erection of the Sphinx."[30]*

That 'lucky turn of the spade' may have already happened. In 1980, Egyptian Egyptologist Zahi Hawass drilled a series of holes to determine the level of the water table, approximately 68 meters east of the Sphinx. After passing through 16 meters of soft debris, the drill hit red quartzite, which is not indigenous to the Giza region. It had to have been imported from the quartzite quarries of the Red Mountain. The Red Mountain was a major quartzite quarry in the Red Hills region of modern Cairo during the Old Kingdom through Middle Kingdom eras. Based on the color and texture of the red quartzite in the Valley Temple, it probably originated in the Red Mountain.

The area Hawass drilled is covered in flood debris

---

[30] Selim Hassan (1949) *The Sphinx: Its history in the light of recent excavation.*

that settled over the region since the quartzite blocks were placed there, however, is significantly lower than the harbor used by the Old Kingdom, and certainly hasn't been exposed since the Old Kingdom. This would imply that someone was building the Giza region significantly earlier than the Old Kingdom, as the water level was high at the time and had been throughout the African Humid Period preceding it. It also means that whatever this red quartzite building is, it dates back to at least 15,000 years ago, and it raises the possibility that the lower level of Khafre's Valley Temple may date back to that time as well.

If the red quartzite lower level of the Khafre Valley Temple does date back to 15,000 years ago, the Sphinx and Sphinx Temple was likely built earlier, as there would have been no reason to transition to building with the inferior stone from the Sphinx enclosure for the new temple. Both temples are also generally built of massive stones aligned at right angles, except for the two walls that are closest to the other temple, which are at an unusual angle. The angle appears to be a continuation of the angle the causeway was built at, however there is no reason the temples should be built this way, as the causeway ends at the red quartzite Valley Temple. The wall of the Valley Temple enclosure is also incomplete on the side bordering the sphinx enclosure, as it could not be fully built because the sphinx temple was in the way. The enclosure wall dates to the 4th dynasty, suggesting that what Khufu found was not the sphinx itself, but the Sphinx Temple, and probably the red quartzite structure that was later expanded under Khafre to become the Valley Temple.

The unusual angle of the temples' walls is also found on the Sphinx enclosure's southern wall, which was carved at a similar, but not identical, angle. Clearly, whatever was obstructing the sphinx enclosure from being completed, it continued west through the space that would later be used for building the red quartzite temple, which resulted in the Sphinx Temple being built at a similar strange angle. This seems to have been a precursor to the causeway, however, not following the exact route of the causeway, as the sphinx enclosure wall is at a slightly different angle. During the 4th dynasty, the two temples were immediately adjacent to the docks, however, the precursor causeway continued, indicating it must have predated the African Humid period, when the water levels in the region were lower.

Naturally, it raises the question of what that precursor causeway was, and where it led. The current causeway leads from the docks to the Mortuary Temple of Khafre at the foot of the pyramid. There are no other obvious remains of an ancient road on the plateau, suggesting the causeway was built where the precursor causeway had been. If so, there must have been something in the vicinity of the Pyramid of Khafre before the pyramid was erected. Unfortunately, if there was anything there before the pyramid was built, it was likely built of the same limestone as the pyramid, and therefore indistinguishable from the rest of the pyramid today.

Unlike the Pyramid of Khufu, the Pyramid of Khafre's interior was simple, and only has the one burial chamber, which is beneath the pink-red granite base. The Pyramid of Khufu also had a subterranean chamber, and therefore, there may have been plans for additional chambers inside the Pyramid of Khafre, however, there is no evidence supporting this. The interior of the Pyramid of Khufu used 8000 tonnes of black granite quarried at Aswan, which is entirely missing from the Pyramid of Khafre.

The third largest pyramid on the plateau, the Pyramid of Menkaure also used a lot of the pink-red granite in its construction. Its exterior lower sixteen courses were made of pink-red granite from Aswan, while the exterior upper courses were made from white Tura limestone. The relative size and placement of the third largest pyramid in relation to the two earlier larger pyramids seems to confirm that Sah had been embraced as the dominant god by the time it was built, as the three pyramids mirror the positions and relative perceived sizes of the stars of Orion's belt.

If the red quartzite temple, the buried red quartzite buildings of the Giza harbor, Osireion of Abydos, which is also made of red quartzite, and underground Labyrinth of the Fayum date to circa 15,000 years ago then this would have been a significant Nile civilization, equivalent in some respects to the later Egyptian Kingdoms. Strabo's account of the upper level of the Labyrinth looking like the Osireion is interesting, as there are no records of the Labyrinth being built. It is assumed to have been built by Amenemhat III, who dug the Grand Canal and built the Pyramid at Hawara, next to the Labyrinth. Amenemhat III was initially building another pyramid, the so-called Black Pyramid at Dahshur, but abandoned that pyramid in order to build the pyramid next to the Labyrinth.

The course of the Grand Canal runs to the west of the area where the underground Labyrinth has been found, however as we do not know exactly how big the structure is, the canal may have broken through the roof of the underground Labyrinth while being dug. It is logical to assume the longer path of the Grand Canal, compared the modern Bahr Wahbi Canal, was due to an obstruction that no longer exists, which raises the possibility that the upper level of the Labyrinth was already there, presumably covered in sediment from the Wild-Nile phase, and was rediscovered by the 12th Dynasty while digging the Grand Canal.

Unfortunately, until the Egyptian government opens the lower level of the Labyrinth for exploration, we may never know what exactly it was. If opened, it should provide samples of ancient debris that could be used to date the Labyrinth, allowing us to know for sure when it was built. While the 30 Kings of Memphis era was the most recent time these archaic structures could have been built, as the water level has been too high ever since, it isn't the earliest time they could have been built. All of these structures could have been built in earlier eras, and may not even date to the same ancient culture. Until we have access to the Labyrinth, we simply cannot know if these sites are actually related, or simply built in similar styles.

1817 Year Line of Kings

Before the 30 kings of Memphis, Manetho listed the rule of another group of kings for 1817 years. Very little is known about this period that apparently existed between approximately 17,280 to 15,463 years ago. This was deep into the glacial drought when Egypt was extremely dry. The period around 17,000 years ago Lake Tana in the Ethiopian highlands dried out, which was the source for 80% of the Nile's water during the later dynastic period. This led to the Nile's water level falling to one of its all-time lowest points. Lake Tana did not recover until sometime after 15,100 years ago.

The other primary source of water for the Nile has traditionally been the White Nile, which flows from Lake Victoria in central Africa. The White Nile is currently the source for around 20% of the Nile's water, however, during the time when Lake Tana was dried out, it would have been the source for most of the Nile's water. However, Lake Victoria was very low at this time as well, ultimately drying out entirely by 15,000 years ago, meaning that the Nile itself, had almost dried out by the end of this very ancient dynasty. It is theorized that the Nile was a seasonal river during this period, flowing only part of the year, and possibly dammed by sand dunes in multiple places where lakes would have formed behind the dams.[31] There is very little that has been discovered dating from this period. Some stone tools have been found along the higher banks of the Nile,

---

[31] Alice Leplongeon (2017) "Technological variability in the Late Palaeolithic lithic industries of the Egyptian Nile Valley: The case of the Silsilian and Afian industries." *PLoS ONE* 12(12): e0188824.

however, the majority of artifacts from this period would likely be buried under the Nile's riverbed, as people would have clustered around the water, not at the top of the surrounding cliffs.

Reign of the Demigods

Before the dynasty of kings that lasted for 1817 years, Manetho listed the rule of the demigods for 1255 years. Whatever this era was about, it apparently existed between approximately 18,535 to 17,280 years ago. This was deep into the glacial drought when Egypt was extremely dry, however, before Lake Tana or Lake Victoria dried out.

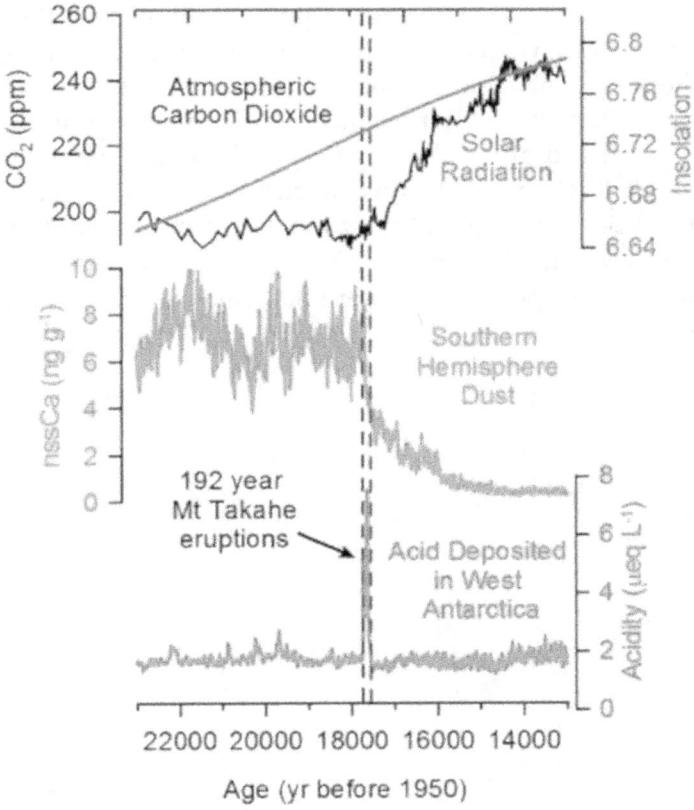

Ice core samples from Antarctica show that between approximately 17,700 and 17,500 years ago, the atmosphere contained a very unusual chemical anomaly of high concentrations of halogens, including chlorine, bromine, and iodine.These halogens were similar to the CFCs emitted by modern civilization in the past century and also created holes in the ozone layer.

The cause of this sudden spike in halogens is theorized to have been a 192-year-long volcanic venting from Mount Takahe in Antarctica. Whatever the demigods were or represented, any remains from the time period along the northern Nile would likely be around 110 meters below the current ground level in the Nile delta. Given the ozone depletion at the time, the reference to demigods could have simply been a memory of people that were deformed by malignant melanoma.

Spirits and Followers of Horus

Prior to the Rule of the Demigods, Manetho claimed there was a 13,900-year-long period where kings ruled, ending with the rule of King Bydis. This corresponds to the 'Spirits and Followers of Horus' listed in the Turin King List, who ruled for 13,420 years. This would have been between approximately 31,955 or 32,435 and 18,535 years ago. This time period generally corresponds to the Last Glacial Maximum (LGM) when the glaciers were at their greatest extent, and the global ocean level was at its lowest point.

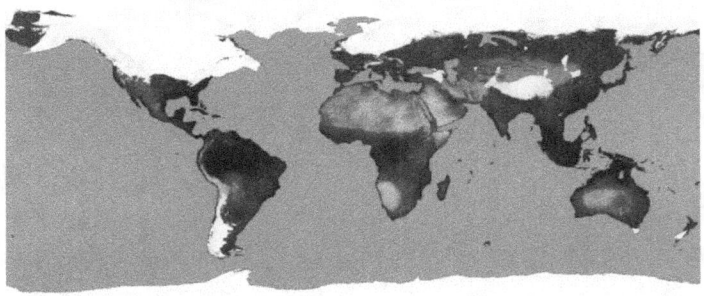

The LGM is generally considered to have existed between 31,000 and 16,000 years ago[32] with its peak circa 26,500 years ago. At the time the world was very dry, and human settlements are believed to have been clustered along the coastlines and riverbanks. Given the fact that the Nile would have been

---

[32] Clare M. Boston (2007) "An examination of the Geochemical properties of late devensian glacigenic sediments in Eastern England, Durham theses'," *Durham E-Theses Online*

significantly lower, probably over 100 meters lower than today, finding any evidence of a culture at the time would be difficult.

Reign of the Gods

Before the reigns of Spirits and Followers of Horus, the Palermo King List stated that there was a time period 23,200 years long that was referred to simply as the Reigns before the Spirits and Followers of Horus. This time period would range from circa 55,155 to 31,955, or 55,635 to 32,435 years ago, depending on whether using the Turin or Manetho King Lists. Manetho broke this period down into the rule of a series of gods, however, did not specify how long each one reigned. The fragments of the Turin King List from that period show the Egyptians of the New Kingdom did believe what Manetho had written over a thousand years later.

One of the few portions of the first two columns of the Turin King List that is still legible is translated as:

The Dual King Djehuty (Thoth), life, prosperity, and health 7726 years.

While Thoth wasn't listed in Manetho's list of gods that ruled, the names of other gods that ruled have been reconstructed from the fragments, including Geb (Column 1.14), Osiris (Column 1.15), Set (Column 1.16), and Horus (Column 1.17). Thoth is mentioned in Column 1.18, followed by Ma'at in Column 1.19, and then Horus again in Column 1.20. The discrepancy between Manetho's list and the Turin List is connected to a religious text that Manetho did not use: the *Book of the Dead*, or as the ancient Egyptians called it: *Book of Coming Forth by Day*.

In the Book of the Dead, Osiris was murdered by Set who became king of Egypt, and raised Osiris' son Horus as his own son, after marrying Osiris widow Isis. Horus ultimately challenged Set in front of a court of gods over-which Thoth presided. The gods decided to uphold Ma'at, which translates as balance, or in context, the law, and restored Horus. This story is believed by Egyptologists to have been created during the Second Intermediate Period when an ethnic Egyptian dynasty was trying to drive out the Asiatic Hyksos dynasty. The story metaphorically illustrated the war in Egypt, where Osiris represented the earlier great Egyptian kingdom that was murdered by the Hyksos, whose patron god was Set. The ethnic Egyptian dynasty was represented by Horus who would eventually be restored to the throne of Egypt by the gods when the rule of law returned to Egypt.

The Turin King List was made during the reign of Ramses II in the New Kingdom when the *Book of the Dead* was the dominant religious text. Thoth, Ma'at, and the second Horus, being added to the list makes political and religious sense as it confirms the authenticity of the *Book of the Dead*. The fact that Manetho didn't include these extra gods likely means that he was using an older source than the Turin King List. As Manetho was a Gnostic and not a follower of any of the ancient Egyptian religions it is unlikely he would see any value in using King Lists that included extra gods that were likely added for political reasons, if he had access to older lists that did not.

Only some of the gods on Manetho's list can be found among the fragments of the Turin papyrus, however, there is clearly several names missing from column one before Geb, and therefore it is plausible that the names Manetho listed were once on the Turin King List. Manetho listed Hephaestus (Ptah), Helios (Ra), Sosis (Shu), Cronos (Geb), Osiris, Typhon (Set), and Orus (Horus) as ruling before the Spirits and Followers of Horus. If the correlation between the 13,900-year-long reign of the kings between Horus and Bydis listed by Manetho, and the 13,420-year-long reign of the 'Spirits and Followers of Horus' is accepted, then the rule of the gods was the 23,200-year-long period before the 'Spirits and Followers of Horus.'

The sequence of gods listed in Manetho's list is clearly drawn from the New Kingdom creation epic of Ptah. In the New Kingdom Ptah became one of the dominant gods, who after building the world passed control of it to the Sun god Ra. After that, the rule of the world passed through the hands of a sequence of gods: Shu, Geb, Osiris, Set, Horus, Thoth, Ma'at, and finally Har. As both Thoth and Ma'at are also listed on the Turin King List, it seems likely that they were added to the king lists of the New Kingdom for religious reasons.

In the Old Kingdom, there was a precursor to the creation epic of Ptah, in the creation epic of Atum. In the creation epic of Atum the rule of the world passed from Atum directly to Shu, and from him onto Geb, Osirus, Set, Horus. Whatever this sequence of gods may represent will likely never be known, and may in fact simply represent a creation myth woven into the ancient Egyptian history.

It appears as if there were once alternate predynastic histories in Egypt, however, we only know about them today because of references to them found in some of the ancient surviving texts. Around 450 BC, Herodotus recorded the history of the Egyptians from the beginning of their civilization, down to the last king before the Assyrians conquered Egypt, a king he called the 'priest of Hephaestus.' After recording the Egyptian dynastic history Herodotus mentioned what came before. Herodotus, Book II, chapters 142 to 144 recounts the following:

"142. Thus far went the record given me by the Egyptians and their priests; and they showed me that the time from the first king to that priest of Hephaestus, who was the last, covered three hundred and forty-one generations of men, and that in this time such also had been the number of their kings, and of their high priests. Now three hundred generations make up ten thousand years, three generations being equal to a century. And over and above the three hundred the remaining forty-one cover thirteen hundred and forty years. Thus the whole sum is eleven thousand three hundred and forty years; in all which time (they said) they had had no king who was a god in human form, nor had there been any such thing either before or after those years among the rest of the kings of Egypt. Four times in this period (so they told me) the sun rose contrary to his wont; twice he rose where he now sets, and twice he set where now he rises; yet Egypt at these times underwent no change, neither in the produce of the river and the land, nor in the matter of sickness and death.

143. *Hecataeus the historian was once at Thebes, where he made for himself a genealogy which connected him by lineage with a god in the sixteenth generation. But the priests did for him what they did for me (who had not traced my own lineage). They brought me into the great inner court of the temple and showed me there wooden figures which they counted up to the number they had already given, for every high priest sets there in his lifetime a statue of himself; counting and pointing to these, the priests showed me that each inherited from his father; they went through the whole tale of figures, back to the earliest from that of him who had lateliest died. Thus when Hecataeus had traced his descent and claimed that his sixteenth forefather was a god, the priests too traced a line of descent according to the method of their counting; for they would not be persuaded by him that a man could be descended from a god; they traced descent through the whole line of three hundred and forty-five figures, not connecting it with any ancestral god or hero, but declaring each figure to be a "Piromis" the son of a "Piromis," that is, in the Greek language, one who is in all respects a good man.*

144. *Thus they showed that all whose statues stood there had been good men, but wholly unlike gods. Before these men, they said, the rulers of Egypt were gods, but none had been contemporary with the human priests. Of these gods one or other had in succession been supreme; the last of them to rule the country was Osiris' son Horus, called by the Greeks Apollo; he deposed Typhon, and was the last divine king of Egypt. In Osiris is in the Greek language, Dionysus."*

The list of gods that are mentioned at the end, Osiris, Horus, and Typhon (Set), are clearly part of the list of gods that reigned in the timeline of Manetho and the Turin Papyrus. According to Herodotus, these gods were not contemporary with human priests, who had recorded the existence of 345 generations of humans during the span of Egyptian history. The Hecataeus mentioned by Herodotus was no doubt the historian and geographer Hecataeus of Miletus, who wrote *Periodos ges* circa 500 BC. These ancient generations apparently added up to 11,340 years, which if then added to the 2500 years since then would place the beginning of these generations circa 13,840 years ago, during the time of the 10 Kings of Thinis, before the Rule of Spirits of the Dead and Demigods. While there is no known evidence of a priestly cast existing through the Wild-Nile Period, it is nevertheless plausible that a cast of priests could have survived in the regions near the Nile during the African Humid Period.

There is evidence of astronomers living in the Sahara during the Wild-Nile Period, at Nabta Playa in southwest Egypt. Nabta Playa is the site of an ancient wetland that existed until the 5.9 Kiloyear Event, where numerous archaeological sites have been discovered dating back to the African Humid Period. Currently, the oldest known human artifacts found at Nabta Playa date to between 10,000 and 8,000 BC.[33]

---

[33] Fred Wendorf and Romuald Schild (November 26, 2000) *Late Neolithic megalithic structures at Nabta Playa (Sahara), south-western Egypt*

Nabta Playa Stone Circle

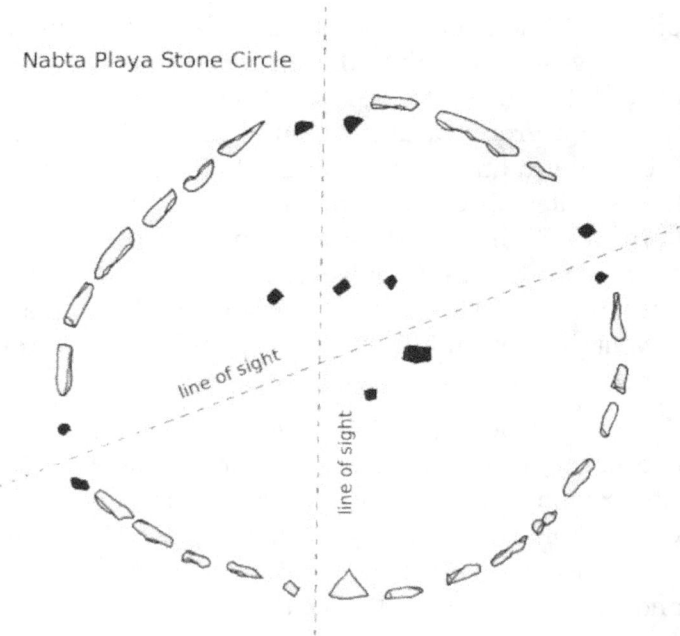

At Nabta Playa are a number of stone circles and aligned standing stones that appear to be ancient star calendars. The most famous is a group of small standing stones that appear to be a star calendar, like a small scale stone henge. These star calendars have been a source of much debate among scholars, with different scholars correlating the calendars with different stars at different points in time. The growing consensus is that the star calendars align with Sirius and Orion circa 6000-6500 BC.

In 2005 astrophysicists Thomas Brophy and Paul Rosen showed that the standing stone orientations and star positions were pointing towards Sirius circa 6088 BC. At the time Sirius had a declination of -36.51 degrees for a rising azimuth, which is where on the C-line average points. The C-line is a line of standing stones within the calendar that has been central to much debate. Near the calendar circle, there is a group of aligned large megalithic stones, the southern line of which aligns to the same stars as the smaller calendar, however, at approximately 6270 BC. Both of these star calendars could also be aligned with Orion, however, in the much larger window of 6400 to 4900 BC. Carbon dated remains of a campfire near the group of megaliths confirm this general timeline, of circa 6000 BC.[34]

It should be noted that while this is the growing consensus, it is not the only proposed dates for the site. Brophy has also pointed out in his book 'The Origin Map' that the alignments at Nabta Playa are also consistent with the alignment of the Milky Way, and Orion, between 17,500 and 16,500 years ago. Orion is the only modern constellation known to have been viewed as an asterism by the ancient Egyptians as early as the Old Kingdom. During the Old Kingdom, circa 4945 to 4003 BC ULT (or 2686 to 2181 BC CET), Orion was known as Sah, 'the father of the gods.' His wife was Sopdet, the star we call Sirius, and their child was the falcon god Sopdu, the planet Venus. These gods were syncretized with Osiris, Isis, and Horus during the First Egyptian Dark Age, which again points to how long that dark age lasted. However, in the Old Kingdom, this triad clearly represented a calendar.

Venus and Earth have orbits around the Sun that

---

[34] G. A. Brophy and P. A. Rosen (2005) "Satellite Imagery Measures of the Astronomically Aligned Megaliths at Nabta Playa," *Mediterranean Archaeology and Archaeometry*, 5 (1): 15–24.

causes Venus to realign with the stars exactly the same every 8 Earth years. This means that the ancients could reset their calendars every 8 years, which happens to be 13 Venusian orbits around the Sun, and thereby keep their calendars in sync with the seasons. This Earth/Venus orbital co-synchronicity was known to the ancient Mesopotamians and Mesoamericans who both used it to reset their calendars every 8 years. Sirius was also known in Egypt as the star which predicted the annual flooding of the Nile, and as such was used to predict the seasons. Once a year, for approximately five days, Sirius would rise right before dawn, which is referred to as the Heliacal Rising of Venus. This happened right before the annual flooding of the Nile, which was caused by the beginning of the wet season in Ethiopia, where most of the Nile water started out.

Herodotus also claimed that the Egyptian priests who had recorded the 345 generations of humans had also claimed that during the entire length of Egyptian history, including the reign of the gods, "Four times in this period (so they told me) the sun rose contrary to his wont; twice he rose where he now sets, and twice he set where now he rises." This is a clear reference to the passage of long spans of time. In Herodotus' time, the Sun was rising in Cancer during the Heliacal Rising of Sirius, approximately July 14-19. The Sun setting Cancer during days of the Heliacal Rising of Sirius would have been 12,960 years earlier. This is due to what astronomers call the precession of the equinoxes.

The precession of the equinoxes is an observable shifting of the constellations over a span of around 25,920 years, during which time the constellations appear to slowly rotate around the earth. Astronomers call it the precession of the equinoxes because Eurasian cultures were more concerned with predicting the course of winter than the heat of summer, however, the ancient Egyptians were more concerned with the summer heat, and the inevitable flooding of the Nile.

If it is accurate that "twice he [the Sun] rose where he now sets, and twice he set where now he rises," then that would refer to a span of time about 51,840 years long, starting approximately 2,450 years ago, when Herodotus wrote it down. In other words, the reign of the gods began approximately 54,290 years ago according to the priests Herodotus spoke with, and around 55,155 to 55,635 years ago according to Manetho and the Turin Papyrus. Whatever this time was supposed to represent, it clearly meant something to the ancient Egyptians.

Conclusion

The current timeline of dynastic Egypt is impossible. Believing in it means endorsing the idea the Hyksos were time-travelers, and that the Egyptians were technologically a thousand years behind their major trading partners in Mesopotamia during the Middle Kingdom. It also is not what the ancient Egyptians actually recorded, so believing it means believing that modern Egyptologists know more about ancient Egypt than the ancient Egyptians themselves. Given that the ancient Egyptians lived through it, and all Egyptologists have to go on is random bits of pottery and mostly ruined buildings, this seems like an incredible stretch of the imagination, granted no more than time-traveling Hyksos, but still a stretch. The fact that Egyptologists feel they don't need to explain these anachronisms because the history of Egypt is a political timeline, not subject to science, is insulting both to the intelligence and to the integrity of anyone that bothers looking into the history of this preeminent ancient culture.

The idea that the ancient Egyptians built docks in the middle of the desert, and then dredged out mind-boggling amounts of mud to move the Nile to the docks, is beyond ridiculous. Maybe that's how Egyptologists would do it, but the existence of the pyramids proves the ancient Egyptians just weren't that stupid. The fact that they did dredge mind-boggling amounts of mud simply proves that the Nile water-levels were dropping rapidly at the end of the Old Kingdom. The fact that Egyptologists ignore the ancient Egyptian records of the pre-Dynastic era is probably for the best, imagine the nonsense they would have made up to explain the Osireion if they had to admit it is 15,000 years old! Wait... let me guess... time-travelers?

Unfortunately, the timeline of Egypt is the cornerstone of ancient history. As the Sumerian and later Mesopotamian civilizations were trading with the Egyptians, the Mesopotamian timeline is broken as the dates of certain Egyptians Kings are known to have lived at the same time as certain Mesopotamian Kings. This means that the bulk of the recorded history of Sumer has to be ignored by Assyriologists, as it just doesn't fit into the Egyptian timeline. As the Harappan history is then dated according to when they were trading with the Mesopotamians, and Indologists also fall subject to the inventive nonsense of Egyptologists. This means that Indologists have to accept the impossible fact that the bronze age Harappan civilization existed next to the iron age Ganges civilization for over 500 years, and never noticed they were there. These broken timelines then fan out further pulling the Minoans and Greeks, Iranians, and Chinese into this confusing mess.

Egyptologists haven't just stolen the real history of Egypt from us, they've stolen the real history of the world from us.

Also Available